TEACHERS WITHOUT GOALS

STUDENTS WITHOUT PURPOSES

TEACHERS WITHOUT GOALS

STUDENTS WITHOUT PURPOSES

HENRY J. PERKINSON

McGraw-Hill, Inc.

New York St. Louis San Francisco Auckland Bogotá Caracas
Lisbon London Madrid Mexico Milan Montreal New Delhi
Paris San Juan Singapore Sydney Tokyo Toronto

This book was developed by Lane Akers, Inc.

TEACHERS WITHOUT GOALS/
STUDENTS WITHOUT PURPOSES

1 2 3 4 5 6 7 8 9 0 FGR FGR 9 0 9 8 7 6 5 4 3 2

ISBN 0-07-049372-3

This book was set in Palatino by The Clarinda Company.
The editor was Lane Akers;
the production supervisor was Al Rihner.
The cover was designed by Carol Couch.
Arcata Graphics/Fairfield was printer and binder.

Library of Congress Cataloging-in-Publication Data

Perkinson, Henry J.
Teachers without goals, students without purposes/Henry J. Perkinson.
p. cm.
ISBN 0-07-049372-3
1. Critical pedagogy. 2. Learning, Psychology of. 3. Teaching.
I. Title.
LC196.P47 1993
371.1'02—dc20 92-26491

About the Author

Henry J. Perkinson is Professor of Educational History at New York University. He is the author of *The Imperfect Panacea: American Faith in Education*; *Learning from Our Mistakes: A Reinterpretation of 20th Century Educational Theories*; and *Getting Better: Television and Moral Progress*. He is former president of the History of Education Society and editor of *The History of Education Quarterly*. He is the recipient of the Distinguished Teacher Award from New York University and of the first Professor of the Year Award given by the School of Education.

A human being who strives for something great considers everyone he meets on his way as a means or as a delay and obstacle—or as a temporary resting place.

Nietzsche

Contents

Preface

As the twentieth century winds down and the crisis in education heats up, it is time to step back and examine our conceptions of education: What kind of transaction are we engaged in? What is the role of the teacher, the student, and the subject matter in this transaction?

These are perennial questions that we should continually discuss but for too long have ignored. Most teachers today continue to accept the answers first put forward in the seventeenth century. This, I believe, has led to our present crisis in education. Some teachers, dissatisfied with the traditional answers, have moved into the realm of nihilism. This further deepens the crisis.

In this brief book, I propose an alternative construction of education, one whose main idea is contained in the book's offbeat title. My purpose is to renew the conversation about these perennial questions. Although I do believe that we teachers never know what we are doing (we can never know all the consequences of our actions), I also believe that we can get better (we can reduce some of the bad consequences of our actions) if we talk to one another.

For many years I have benefited from participating in this endless conversation with my friends and colleagues, Neil

Postman and Chris Nystrom. In this book, fellow-teachers Peter Airasian, Joan Burstyn, and Joel Spring add their voices to the conversation. I hope you will, too.

Whenever I have mentioned the title of this book to anyone, I am met with knowing nods and muttered agreement: "Yeah, right! That's what's wrong with schools. Teachers have no goals; students have no purposes." I usually have difficulty convincing people that I propose this as the solution to what is wrong with schools: teachers *should* have no goals; students *should* have no purposes.

I make this quirky recommendation because I have come to the conclusion that contemporary educational practice is based on a thoroughly incorrect theory of knowledge. Most teachers have a completely inadequate conception of the nature of knowledge: of where knowledge comes from and of how it grows. Besides corrupting the practice of education, this incorrect theory of knowledge has made improvement impossible. As Michael Oakeshott has noted, "The practical danger of an erroneous theory is not that it may persuade people to act in an undesirable manner, but that it may confuse activity by putting it on a false scent."

In this book, I sketch an alternative approach to education, a critical approach based on the theory of knowledge that Sir Karl Popper calls evolutionary epistemology. Even if this critical approach to teaching proves inadequate, my hope is that the theory of knowledge on which it is based may help put educators on the right scent.

In the book, I contrast the critical approach to education with other approaches that I label modern, postmodern, and post-postmodern approaches. Readers should not take these terms too seriously. I have not grounded them in the ever-burgeoning literature that these terms have generated. I use them here only as labels to sort out different approaches to teaching. What I mean by the terms will be clear from the text itself.

Henry J. Perkinson

TEACHERS WITHOUT GOALS

STUDENTS WITHOUT PURPOSES

PART ONE

AGAINST MODERNISM

1

Against Learning

I am not really against learning (who could be?), but against teachers viewing their jobs as the promotion of learning. As I see it, there are a number of problems with construing teaching this way. The basic difficulties spring from the "commonsense" belief, shared by most people, that learning comes from without. Although this receptacle, or bucket, theory of learning goes back to Aristotle, it is the basis for the modern approach to teaching. Most modern teachers see their jobs as filling up the students' bucketlike minds by "transmitting" knowledge to them.

THE MODERN THEORY OF EDUCATION

Modernism, as I am using the term, began with Francis Bacon, who revived the Aristotelian notion that we receive knowledge through our senses by insisting that the growth of scientific knowledge takes place through induction. Scientists, he said, draw general conclusions from the observation of many particulars. Instead of reading books in search of knowledge, Bacon told us we should read the book of nature. If we observe nature directly, unhampered by prejudices, traditions, fashions—what he calls "idols"—then we will grasp true knowledge. This notion that truth is manifest, that human beings can grasp it with certainty, became the basis for modern universal education. According to this theory, teachers can "transmit" knowledge to everyone simply by presenting to their students the world, the real world, so that they can grasp it through their senses.

The first modern educator was probably John Amos Comenius, who, in a series of books he composed during the seventeenth century—including *The World through Sense Pictures* and *The Great Didactic*—developed methods for teaching "all things to all people . . . quickly, thoroughly, and pleasantly." As Comenius saw it, the effective "transmission" of knowledge required teachers to package it properly into digestible portions so that students, after being themselves prepared and motivated by the teacher, could readily receive it.

After a century or so, however, theorists like Rousseau complained that students were not really receiving the knowledge transmitted to them. As Rousseau saw it, Comenius (and Aristotle, and Locke, and most philosophers) had erred in conceiving the mind as a bucket to be filled, or as a blank sheet of paper upon which the teacher imprinted knowledge. He reminded teachers that human beings grow and develop over time. Teachers, he complained, wrongly concentrate on what "it is important for men to know without consulting what children are in a condition to learn. They are always seeking the man in the child without thinking of what he is before being a man." To be effective, Rousseau argued, teachers must pay heed to the stages of development all children go through and transmit to them only that knowledge they are *ready* to receive.

By the end of the next century, the nineteenth, John Dewey had taken the insights of Rousseau and combined them with the theory of evolution to come up with the notion that learning takes place through the solving of problems. That is, if the species evolved, or grew, by solving problems of adaptation to a continuously changing environment, then, Dewey argued, we can say that organisms *learned* to adapt. Thus, learning is a matter of solving problems one encounters in pursuit of ends or goals. As Dewey saw it, students do not receive knowledge; they discover it. The trick that teachers now had to pull off consisted of confronting students with problems in accord with their level of development, but problems that would, at the same time, enable them to discover the knowledge the teacher wanted them to learn. Although Dewey's theory construed the student as an active discoverer rather than a passive receptor, his construction of education remains very much in line with the traditional, Aristotelian, notion that we receive knowledge from without.

AN ALTERNATIVE THEORY

An alternative exists to the notion that knowledge comes from without, an alternative that goes back to Socrates and Plato, both of whom maintained that knowledge comes from within—from the knower. This conception has some life at present insofar as two eminent twentieth-century psychologists, B. F. Skinner and Jean Piaget, both subscribed to it. Yet this notion that knowledge comes from the learner sharply contradicts the modern view that has been part of "common sense" since the seventeenth century. Understandably, then, both Skinner and Piaget have met strong resistance and much misunderstanding of their theories.

The modern conception of learning is so deeply entrenched that I find I am against learning; that is, I am against treating education as the promotion of learning. Instead, I suggest that we consider education as growth, the growth of knowledge. By construing education in this way, we can escape from the long and deep spell that Aristotle's bucket theory of learning has cast over education. Our best theory of how growth takes place is the theory of evolution, of which Aristotle knew nothing. In short, I propose that we construe education as the evolution of knowledge.

Many teachers already talk about education as growth, but most see it in pre-Darwinian terms—as the accumulation of knowledge from without. The growth of knowledge, as they view it, simply consists of filling the mind with ideas, facts, theories, and other mental entities. John Dewey did, of course, profess to have an evolutionary theory of the growth of knowledge, but he, too, gave it an Aristotelian twist by adopting Lamarck's theory of evolution. Jean-Baptiste Lamarck (1744–1829) believed that the species evolved through the process of solving problems of adaptation. By solving such problems, organisms acquired characteristics that they then transmitted biologically to their progeny. Thus, the giraffe acquired its long neck, according to the Lamarckians, when its ancestors solved the problem of securing leaves from the topmost branches of trees by stretching their necks. They then transmitted long necks to their offspring. In time, the story goes, all giraffes had long necks. Consonant with Lamarck's theory, Dewey maintained that human beings acquire (discover) knowledge by solving problems and then transmit this knowledge to the young via instruction. This is a replay of the conventional transmission theory of education. In applying this theory to the classroom, Dewey proposed that teachers transmit knowledge to students by posing problems in a way that would allow the students to *discover* what they were supposed to learn.

Almost all biologists today reject Lamarck's theory in favor of Darwin's theory of evolution. I suggest that all teachers should likewise reject Dewey's theory of growth.

What would a Darwinian theory of education look like? For one thing, it would expunge from education the notion that teachers must have goals, as well as the belief that they must pay heed to their students' purposes.

2

Students without Purposes

At least once a semester, one of my students—all of whom are practicing or future teachers—will tell me that you cannot make somebody learn who doesn't want to learn. "You can lead a horse to water, but you can't make him drink," the more philosophically minded point out. When I tell them that this argument hinges on the notion that we acquire knowledge from without, they look confused. "Where else could knowledge come from?" they ask.

This notion, that we acquire knowledge from without, is, I think, the single most wrong-headed belief shared by most teachers. Those who subscribe to it render themselves ineffectual teachers.

First of all, the notion that we are receptors of knowledge, that we acquire knowledge from without, cannot explain why some people fail to learn what the teacher has taught. "The students failed to pay attention" is the lame excuse usually proffered. (Do teachers still ask students to "keep their eyes and ears open"!) Or maybe the student did not learn because he or she has an impaired receptor apparatus—"learning disabled" is the term one usually hears. Yet all about us we have physically impaired students—the blind and the deaf, for example—successfully learning. How do these students learn?

The fact is that human beings are not receptors of knowledge. We are not like radios, or television sets, or tape recorders—receptors that never make a mistake, receptors that always receive the messages transmitted. If we were receptors, then *surely* we would be better receptors than the radios, television sets, or tape recorders we ourselves construct. So, since we make mistakes in "receiving" knowledge "transmitted" to us, it seems likely that human beings do not receive knowledge.

Then where does knowledge come from? My answer is that it comes from us. Human beings create their knowledge. We decode, or construct, or *make* sense of whatever we encounter. And we do this by creating theories about, or understandings of, whatever we encounter.

But if human beings do create their knowledge, my ever-critical students argue, then how can this explain why students do learn what is taught? Why does each student not create his or her own idiosyncratic understanding of what the teacher presents?

My answer is that there is a real world, a world that "kicks back." This "negative feedback" from the real world reveals when one has come up with an understanding that does not "fit." Thus, the growth of knowledge is a process of adaptation. Knowledge that survives is the knowledge that "fits." Indeed, the notion that we create our knowledge rather than receive it from without comes from a theory of knowledge called evolutionary epistemology. Developed by Karl Popper and others, evolutionary epistemology is an attempt to use Darwin's theory of evolution to explain the growth of knowledge.

EVOLUTIONARY EPISTEMOLOGY

According to Darwin, the evolution, or growth, of the species took place through natural selection. "The principle of preservation, or the survival of the fittest, I have called Natural Selection," Darwin wrote. "It leads to the improvement of each creature in relation to its organic and inorganic conditions of life; and consequently, in most cases, to what may be regarded as an advancement in organization." According to this theory, organisms, over time, gave birth to offspring that varied slightly from themselves. Nature selected those that were unfit and eliminated them. Those that survived had, in time, offspring that varied slightly from themselves. And once again, nature eliminated those that were unfit. Evolution, then, is a process of trial-and-error elimination: organisms create trial offspring, and nature eliminates the errors, those that are inadequate or unfit. Through the process of natural selection, new species evolved from those that already existed.

Evolutionary epistemologists argue that knowledge evolves through the same process of selection, the same process of trial-and-error elimination. According to these theorists, as organisms not only do we create biological offspring, but we also create knowledge—skills and understandings.

At this point, it is necessary to explain what evolutionary epistemologists mean by knowledge. What is the nature of knowledge? As they view it, knowledge consists of theories, or conjectures, or guesses. It is, I think, not too difficult to see that our understandings of the past, say, our understanding of the thirteenth century, consist of conjectures, or guesses. This is not to deny that some people have better conjectures (or understandings) than others—i.e., some people's conjectures fit better with the facts. Similarly, we can readily construe our understandings of the physical universe, say, the orbiting of the planets, as conjectures, too. So, one can fairly easily accept the notion that all human understandings are conjectures, or hypotheses. But for evolutionary epistemologists, this holds for skills, too, and holds for our organs as well, especially our organs of perception. Our skills and our organs, like our eyes, for example, are embodied theories about the world we inhabit—theories embodied in actions (skills), or theories embodied in our physiological structures (organs).

Take the eye, for example. The spectrum of light waves perceivable by the eye is but a small slice of the entire electromagnetic spectrum. Thus, the eye is an embodied theory about what is "out there." Or take the lowly paramecium. When it collides with an obstacle, the paramecium reverses its movements and swims in another direction. The paramecium has an innate theory about its environment which takes the form of anticipations: some objects are impenetrable; collisions can be avoided by backing up and swimming off in a new direction. This knowledge is the result of evolution or of the contingencies of survival: only those organisms born with this understanding—disposed to act this way—survived. Yet this inborn knowledge is never perfect; what an organism anticipates can never be certain knowledge. A frog, for example, is so constituted that it can see its prey—a fly—only when the fly moves. When the fly sits still, the frog cannot see it, even if the fly is very close: the frog's knowledge of its prey is not the result of observation. Rather, it is the other way around. What the frog observes—the prey it sees—is the result of the theory embedded in its eye: a prey (fly) is something that moves.

So animals, as well as humans, have knowledge. And animal knowledge, like human knowledge, is conjectural; it comes from the organism, not from without, and it grows through trial-and-error elimination. Popper is fond of saying that there is only one step from the amoeba to Einstein. Of course, Einstein's knowledge, human knowledge, is better knowledge than that created by the amoeba—better insofar as it is more universal, better adapted to the environment. This is so, in part, because humans have more complex organs than the amoeba, organs that, through the power of natural selection, are better adapted to the environment.

Consider the tick. The tick survives by feeding on mammals, which means that it must "know" a mammal when it encounters one. The tick is programmed to let itself fall from a twig when it "smells" butyric acid and to cling to an object provided the object has a temperature of 37 degrees Celsius. Thus, the tick's "understanding," or "theory," of a mammal is incomplete, less universal than that of more complex animals. As Peter Munz notes: "It is easier to simulate a mammal to mislead a tick than it is to simulate a mammal to mislead a human being."*

*Peter Munz, *Our Knowledge of the Growth of Knowledge: Popper or Wittgenstein* (London: Routledge & Kegan Paul, 1985), p. 247.

Moreover, not only are complex organisms better adapted than ticks, but complex organisms (like animals and human beings) can use their organs, their sensory organs, to *create* theories about the environment—theories about how various objects smell, taste, look, sound, and feel, as well as theories about what can be done with and to objects in the environment. Over time, as the result of continuous trial-and-error elimination, complex organisms do construct a repertoire of knowledge about the environment they inhabit. This is subjective knowledge, knowledge that is embedded in the body of the organism, kinesic knowledge. And although both animals and humans have knowledge, humans have superior knowledge, knowledge that better "fits."

The greatest evolutionary advantage that human beings have over all other organisms is that they can encode their knowledge in language—in speech, in writing, in print. Because of this, human knowledge can become objective knowledge—knowledge that exists *apart* from a knowing subject. When knowledge is encoded in language, when it has an objective existence apart from us, we can discuss it and criticize it. Thus, we can uncover errors and inadequacies in our theories without actual physical trial-and-error elimination. When knowledge is encoded in language, we can test and improve it via critical discussion. Moreover, when it is encoded in language, human knowledge becomes objective knowledge. Objective knowledge, unlike the subjective, kinesic, knowledge of other organisms, takes on a life of its own. There is a "body" of human knowledge called physics, another called history, another called mathematics, and so on. Human beings have created these bodies of knowledge, and like the biological bodies human beings also create—their children—these various bodies of knowledge evolve and grow—so much so that we can compose and have composed histories of the growth and development of bodies of knowledge: histories of mathematics, histories of science, etc.

As the evolutionary epistemologists have made clear, the growth of these bodies of objective knowledge in every field follows the Darwinian process of trial-and-error elimination. In physics, for example, physicists have made conjectures about the physical universe. These conjectures are encoded in language—in speech or writing or print. Thus objectified, these conjectures can be discussed and criticized by other physicists. When criticism uncovers inadequacies in these conjectures the theories are modified or sometimes rejected outright, and they are replaced by other, better, theories—better insofar as they are not open to the same criticisms. In time, critics uncover inadequacies in these new theories, too, which leads to their modification or perhaps rejection and replacement by still better theories. This growth through trial-and-error elimination takes place continually in every field of human knowledge, as scholars and researchers subject the present state of their field to continuous criticism and to refinement in the light of the inadequacies uncovered by criticism.

THE GROWTH OF PERSONAL HUMAN KNOWLEDGE

Without subscribing to the dictum "ontogeny recapitulates phylogeny," evolutionary epistemologists argue that each human being's personal knowledge evolves or grows in the same way as the knowledge of any given field grows: through trial-and-error elimination—trial, or conjectured, theories are held up to criticism, which uncovers inadequacies. The elimination of these inadequacies improves the theories.

In explaining how the growth of personal human knowledge takes place, evolutionary epistemologists point to the fact that human beings, like all organisms, have an inborn expectation of order, or, to put it negatively, an inborn aversion to disorder. Thus, a sudden flash of light, a loud noise, a fall—startles us, upsets us. As does a rebuke, an unexpected answer, an unanticipated outcome. This aversion to disorder, to disequilibration, is clearly a contingency of survival, for organisms could not long survive if they were to tolerate disorder, incoherence, and contradictions. It is this aversion to disorder that makes the growth of knowledge possible, since it is this aversion to disorder that makes organisms modify or refine their actions when the results are not as anticipated. In other words, it is we who impose order on the world, or on our experiences of the world. We *literally* make sense of the world. We do not *observe* order; we do not discover order or intuit it; we impose order on the world. We construct theories that make sense of what we encounter. When we find out that these theories are not adequate, do not fit, we become disequilibrated, which leads us to modify, refine, change them. We improve them.

At any given moment—from birth onward—humans, like all other organisms, have theories that lead to, or take the form of, expectations. The totality of these expectations makes up what can be called one's horizon of expectations, a cognitive map the organism uses to negotiate its way in the world. Yet our maps, or theories—including those we are born with—are not reliable; our expectations are often disappointed. This, however, leads to growth, to the modification and improvement of our theories and, therefore, to changes in our horizon of expectations.

What is important to note is that in the growth of knowledge, as in the evolution of the species, there is no purpose. In biological evolution, organisms do not adapt to the environment because of some "purpose," or some motivation; adaptation takes place through blind trial-and-error eliminations. In the case of the evolution of knowledge, as well as in the evolution of the species, organisms are creators; they create offspring, and they create knowledge; evolution, or growth, takes place through the elimination of what is not fit, the elimination of errors and mistakes in what was created. This elimination of errors results in the modification or refinement through subsequent trial creations. If the parallel that evolutionary epistemologists make between the growth of knowledge and the growth or evolution of the species is correct, then students' purposes are irrelevant to the growth of their knowledge. Students' knowledge *will* grow; *students will* improve it when they recognize inadequacies in what they heretofore accepted as adequate.

GROWTH WITHOUT PURPOSE

A newborn baby has a disposition to suck everything that comes into or near her mouth. The baby expects to be nourished. She has a theory about the relation between the world and herself: the world is for sucking. But through repeated trial-and-error elimination, the baby modifies her sucking behavior: some things do not taste as anticipated; so the baby modifies her theory—only some things are for sucking. This theory creates a new order, or restores order, in the infant's understanding of the world. Of course, the new theory is not perfect. Yet it is a better theory than the baby's first theory, one better adapted to the universe the baby inhabits. The infant still tries to suck some things that do not provide nourishment, and may even be lethal. Yet we should not regard our adult theories about what is to be sucked and what not as perfect theories; for although adults usually do have theories better adapted to the world than those of infants, adult theories are not perfect, either. Human knowledge is fallible—it can always be improved.

Human infants continually modify their sensorimotor acts in the light of disappointed expectations. These modifications constitute improvements in the child's knowledge: the child learns how better to grasp objects—small objects, large ones, and fragile ones, too; learns how better to crawl, creep, walk, and run, as well as how better to look, listen, smell, and taste. As we know from observing athletes, wine tasters, and connoisseurs of all types, level of performance can be improved continually throughout one's lifetime. Some people, of course, have more "natural" talent than others in sensorimotor skills and so can more readily attain high levels of performance. But the process through which these "naturals" improve their performance is the same as for the rest of us: trial-and-error elimination.

After the sensorimotor stage of development, the second, and most particularly human, stage in the growth of personal knowledge begins when the child begins to speak.* Speech al-

*Here readers will recognize that I am following—in an admittedly loose way—the widely accepted stages of development proposed by Jean Piaget.

THE FUNCTIONS OF LANGUAGE

		Function	Values	
		4. Argumentative function	Validity/ invalidity	Humans
	Perhaps bees	3. Descriptive function	Falsity/truth	Humans
	Perhaps bees	2. Signal function	Efficiency/ inefficiency	Humans
Animals, plants	Perhaps bees	1. Expressive function	Revealing/not revealing	Humans

Source: Karl Popper and John Eccles, *The Self and the Brain* (New York: Springer, 1977), p. 58.

lows human beings to encode their theories in language. Other organisms are capable of making sounds that *express* inner feelings: fear, contentment, hunger, sexual desire, etc.; and many other organisms can make sounds that serve as *signals:* "danger," "food," "come," "go," "stop," etc. But only humans can speak, and thereby use sounds to *describe:* to describe persons, places, and things, as well as events, happenings, and goings on. When the child begins to speak—by which I mean to use language to describe and not merely to express feelings or to signal—the regulative idea of truth emerges: description that fits the facts.*

With the development of speech and the emergence of the regulative idea of truth, a fourth function of language emerges: the argumentative function. The emergence of this function accelerates the growth of human knowledge. Growth still takes place through the process of trial-and-error elimination, but now it becomes possible to criticize theories by critically discussing them, to uncover their inadequacies, mistakes, errors, without actually acting on them. With speech, logic becomes the organ of criticism. Once they begin to speak, children use logic to uncover the inadequacies of their theories, or recognize inadequacies when logical arguments are presented to them. However, as

*It may be that bees, dolphins, and some primates can use language to describe, as well as to signal and express, but the problem of lying does not arise; animals do not lie; hence, no regulative idea of truth emerges.

Piaget has demonstrated, although young children can use speech argumentatively, the grasp of logic only develops over time.

If human knowledge grows through the process of trial-and-error elimination, then this is how students learn in school. It is how they learn to read and to write; how they learn to type, to swim, to sew; and how they learn history, physics, Latin, and biology. All learning is the modification of the knowledge—the modification of the skills and understandings—one already possesses. Learning, or growth, is up to the student; it is the student who must modify, or refine, his or her existing knowledge when he or she recognizes its inadequacies.

So in spite of what my students tell me every semester, purposes are not necessary to learning; students do not have to want to learn in order for their knowledge to grow. Note that I do not deny that students, like all human beings, have purposes. What I deny is that teachers must pay heed to students' purposes in order to teach them, in order to promote the growth of their knowledge. Indeed, it is this mistaken belief that has crippled schooling. It has trivialized the content of education and subverted our methods of teaching. This mistaken belief stems from the wrong-headed notion that knowledge comes to us from without, which makes teachers erroneously conclude that they can be transmitters of knowledge and that they can better transmit knowledge if they pay attention to their students' purposes. If the alternative conception of the growth of knowledge proposed by evolutionary epistemology is correct, then knowledge does not, ever, come to us from without, and transmission does not, cannot, exist. So there is no reason to pay heed to students' purposes.

If teachers do not, cannot, transmit knowledge to students, what are teachers for? What role do teachers play in the educational transaction?

3

Teachers without Goals

THE ARGUMENT AGAINST GOALS

Ever since Aristotle, people have tried to explain the goings-on in the universe by reference to goals, or purposes, or ends. Following the birth of modern science in the seventeenth century, however, we have gradually abandoned the teleological explanations of the physical world. We do not say that ice cubes *intend* to melt, nor that planets *want* to revolve around the sun in an ellipse, nor that stones fall because they *seek* their proper resting place. But most of us still try to explain human conduct teleologically, by reference to purposes or goals. Harking back to Aristotle—"Every act and every investigation and similarly every action and pursuit, is considered to aim at some good"—we believe that every rational activity aims at some end, or good.

So it is with teachers. Most teachers approach their task by identifying goals or aims. Indeed, most teachers not only see each lesson and each class in terms of goals; this is how they see the entire educational process: as an enterprise, a mission, a journey toward some end.

Teachers usually couch their goals in terms of what they want the students to learn, what knowledge they want students to acquire. As they see it, their role is to transmit the targeted knowledge to the students. As noted before, this construction of the educational transaction arises from the belief that we acquire knowledge from without, the belief that the mind is a bucket to be filled with knowledge.

But if the argument presented in the preceding chapter is correct, we are not passive receptors of knowledge; rather, we are active, although fallible, creators of knowledge. And we create new knowledge when we uncover inadequacies in our present knowledge. In every case, the growth of knowledge consists of modifying the knowledge one already possesses.

From this, it follows that teachers cannot transmit knowledge to students. It may *look* as though the teacher is transmitting knowledge to students, but this is an illusion. A teacher can present knowledge to students, but it is the students who create their understandings of what the teacher presents. And the understanding each student creates is largely a product of the knowledge the student already possesses. In the language of Piaget, students assimilate what the teacher presents—by which he means they *make* sense of it in accord with the knowledge they already have. This frequently results in errors and misapprehensions of what the teacher presents. On the other hand, some students do create a reasonable facsimile of what the teacher has presented, and can reproduce it—for a test, say.

Thus, although the transmission of knowledge is an illusion, it is the case that teachers can and do *try* to transmit knowledge. But transmission does not occur; instead, in every case, it is the students who create their understandings of what the teacher presents. And even though students do sometimes create reasonable facsimiles of what the teacher wants them to learn, the attempt to transmit knowledge to students corrupts education.

First of all, it is immoral for teachers to do this. When they attempt to transmit knowledge, teachers have to ignore their own fallibility and, at the same time, deny agency to the students. That is, when they try to transmit knowledge, teachers presume to decide what students should know and to impose that knowledge on them. What actually happens here is that the students are forced, or constrained, to create the understandings that the teacher deems "correct." This converts education into an authoritarian transaction. (But I must note that many teachers—more than I had expected—accept this authoritarianism as an inherent characteristic of education.)

Second, there are pragmatic reasons for not trying to transmit knowledge to students: such attempts usually fail. The student may retain this so-called transmitted knowledge (but actually created knowledge) for a time—until he or she regurgitates it, say, for a test—but such knowledge usually does not take; it usually does not become a permanent part of the student's own knowledge. Such knowledge disappears not, as some claim, because the student does not use it, or because it is irrelevant, or meaningless, to the student. No, such knowledge disappears because it never was the student's *own* knowledge; it was not knowledge the student created by modifying his or her own knowledge. It was knowledge the student created solely to pass the test or to please the teacher. It was "school knowledge," constructed and held apart from the student's *own* knowledge. Hence, it soon disappears.

The final reason for not attempting to transmit knowledge to students is a pedagogic one: it prevents further growth. That is, when attempts to transmit knowledge are seemingly successful, this is usually an indication that the "transmitted" knowledge has become a *true belief* for the student—knowledge that the student will retain tenaciously, knowledge that will not grow. As evidence of this, one need only recall that the most "successful" students in our schools—the ones who learn what the teacher transmits—usually are, or become, the most dogmatic knowers.

FACILITATING THE GROWTH OF KNOWLEDGE

The critical approach to teaching I will describe here avoids the difficulties connected to attempts to transmit knowledge. It holds out the possibilities (1) that education need not be authoritarian, (2) that teachers can facilitate *real* learning by helping students improve their own knowledge, and (3) that education can occur in such a way that students' knowledge will continue to grow.

Education then is not a mission, not a journey to some predetermined end. Education is an adventure. Teachers who adopt the critical approach do not have goals; they have agenda. That is, each teacher focuses on a specific part of a student's knowledge. A teacher may focus on helping students improve their writing, or their mathematical skills, or their understanding of the physical world; this is the teacher's agenda.

What I present here is not original, nor novel. As teachers from Socrates to Montessori have argued, all education is self-education; the student educates himself or herself. The teacher's task is simply to facilitate this self-education. In doing this, the teacher assumes, first, that the student has knowledge; second, that the student's knowledge is inadequate. From these two assumptions, it follows, third, that the student's knowledge is capable of improvement—which is what the educational transaction is all about. But improvement or growth is up to the student. The student is the one who modifies his or her present knowledge. The teacher facilitates growth of knowledge by creating an environment that allows the student to engage in those trial-and-error elimination activities through which growth takes place. Since an educative environment facilitates growth, it is important to examine what characterizes an educative environment.

CREATING AN EDUCATIVE ENVIRONMENT

As I see it, an educative environment must have three aspects: it must be free, critical, and supportive.

A Free Environment

The teacher creates a free environment in order to educe the students' present knowledge: to determine what they know, or can do—their present understandings or skills. Let us suppose the agenda is some skill. The teacher's task is to help students improve their writing, say, or reading, or dancing, or drawing, or boxing, or acting, or singing, or some other skill. Teachers of skills usually view their role as that of a coach. The first order of business for the coach who adopts the critical approach is to find out what the students can do. The teacher-coach does this by creating an environment wherein the students feel free to disclose what they can do, free to disclose their present level of proficiency. A coach creates a free environment by being accepting, not by being judgmental, not by being censorious, and, above all, not by attempting to teach students anything. At this stage of the educational transaction, the teacher merely wants the students to reveal what they can do.

The teacher-coach can elicit the students' present level of proficiency in a variety of ways. The writing teacher, for example, can ask students to write a paragraph or essay. The swimming coach can ask students to get into the pool and swim as fast as they can. The drawing teacher can present a model for students to copy. The typing teacher can demonstrate how to hold one's hands on the keyboard and then invite the students to do the same. The carpentry teacher can assign a project. The singing teacher can propose an exercise. The purpose in all cases is to elicit from the students their present level of proficiency—*not* to show them how to perform some skill. This phase of student disclosure and display should be long enough for the students to become relaxed and comfortable—appreciative of the fact that the teacher accepts what they can do, and does not judge, nor censor, nor grade, their performance. Indeed, the coach should praise these initial student efforts. But the importance of these initial performances—as the teacher should make clear—is to establish a starting point, a benchmark, for ascertaining further improvement. It may be helpful to maintain some permanent record of these initial displays of the students' skills.

Here I might note a mistake many modern teachers of skills make. They construe skills as habits, habits acquired through repetition. These teachers begin by demonstrating the skill and then ask the student to copy or imitate what they have done. The teacher then intervenes to *correct* the student's performance, to see to it that the student does it correctly. This is followed by having the student practice. Through such repetition, the teacher believes, the student will make the skill a part of his or her repertoire.

The argument against such an approach is that the student cannot acquire a *correct* performance of a skill, simply because there is no way of knowing that what works at one time will work in the future. Many will accuse me of quibbling at this point, and say that, yes, logically there can be no certainty, and so the acquired skill might not work in the future because the situation may be different; nevertheless, in the real world, they point out, a skill that works at one time will usually be effective in the future. Yet my argument is not just a quibble: it is a logical argument that shows we do not, cannot, learn skills via repetition. Carl Yastrzemski, the first American League baseball player ever to get 3000 hits, saw this clearly: "I haven't the greatest ability in the world," he explained. "I'm not a big, strong guy. I've made nine million adjustments, nine million changes." Yastrzemski does not say whether he himself uncovered the mistakes and inadequacies that led to these "nine million changes." Probably not. This is what coaches are for, as we shall see.

We do not learn skills by learning the "correct" way to perform them and then repeating this until it becomes a habit. Rather, we learn skills (or improve our performance) through continual trial-and-error elimination. We never learn to perform a skill "correctly"—we can always improve our performance. The teacher who tells students to keep performing a skill in the same way will not help them to improve. For the future is not the past; what worked in the past may not work in the future, in a different situation. So the teacher's role is not to show students how to perform a skill correctly, but rather to help them improve the skills they have. The first stage is to educe the students' skills by creating a free environment.

A Critical Environment

In the second phase of the educational transaction—after having elicited the student's level of proficiency—the teacher who adopts the critical approach helps the students to recognize the mistakes, errors, inadequacies in his or her performance. Here, the teacher-coach becomes a critic or creates a critical environment. Most students have some vague awareness of the inadequacies in their skills but do not know what it is that they are doing wrong. One way the teacher helps them see what they are doing wrong is by getting them to recognize the consequences of what they are actually doing. Thus, "When you draw a house this way, then this is the effect on the viewer"; or "when you write a sentence this way, then this is the effect on the reader"; or "if you hold your arms this way when you box, then these are the consequences." In helping students recognize the unwanted consequences of their actions, teachers can involve other students in the class as collaborators who will help uncover the inadequacies. Many teachers of writing, for example, do employ this collaborative approach.

This critical approach follows a well-known logical form, called *modus tollens*.

$$\begin{array}{ll} (1) & p \supset q \\ (2) & \phantom{p \supset{}} -q \\ \hline (3) & \phantom{p \supset{}} -p \end{array}$$

Let p be the student's performance and q be the anticipated outcome. In statement 1 the student assumes, "If I perform p, then q will follow": $(p \supset q)$. In statement 2 the teacher points out, "q did not follow": $(-q)$. Statement 3 is the conclusion the *student* must draw: "Therefore, p is inadequate": $(-p)$. Thus:

1. "If I swing the bat this way, then the ball will fly to left field."
2. "The ball did not fly to left field."
3. "Therefore, there is something wrong with the way I am swinging the bat."

No matter what skill the teacher-coach wants to help improve, the critical approach is the same: to help the students uncover the unanticipated and unwanted consequences of their present levels of performance. To be effective and not overburden students, teachers should limit attention to just a few particular errors or inadequacies at a time, focusing especially on those of a sort that the student can readily repair.

Here let me note a mistake that many modern teachers of skills make—a mistake that stems from their having goals. The teacher with goals who teaches a skill usually construes the goal as the consequence of a performance. Say the teacher wants the student to hit the ball to left field—this is the goal. When the student does this effectively, the teacher claims to have attained the goal and concludes that the student has learned the skill. Or say the teacher of reading wants the student to learn how to read a complex passage. When the student is able to answer questions, or pass a test, on the given passage, the teacher claims to have attained the goal and concludes that the student has learned the skill. This is a logical error, called "affirming the consequent."

$$\begin{array}{ll} (1) & p \supset q \\ (2) & \quad\;\; q \\ \hline (3) & p \end{array}$$

The conclusion, statement 3, is invalid. In terms of the baseball coach and the student:

1. "If the student swings the bat correctly, then the ball will go to left field": $(p \supset q)$.
2. "The ball goes to left field": (q).
3. "Therefore, the student swung the bat correctly": (p).

But obviously this does not follow. The ball may have flown to left field for any number of reasons, not simply because the student swung the bat the way he did. Moreover, this may have happened because of how that particular pitcher threw that particular pitch, at that particular time, that the student hit to left field. Swinging the same way in a different situation, the student would not have hit the ball to left field. Furthermore, it does not matter how many times, and under how many different situations, the student does hit the ball to left field; one cannot logically conclude that the student has swung the bat correctly. You cannot deduce a true conclusion by affirming the consequent.

You can try this out with any number of examples:

> If I throw this punch correctly, then my opponent will be knocked down.
> My opponent was knocked down.
> Therefore, I threw the punch correctly.

Obviously, the conclusion is invalid.

> If I write a funny story, then people will smile when they read it.
> They smiled when they read my story.
> Therefore, I wrote a funny story.

Another invalid conclusion, alas.

The general point to be made here is to remind educators of human fallibility. Students can never have perfect skills; whatever the level of their proficiency may be, they can always improve. So in teaching skills, the teacher who adopts the critical approach does not teach students new skills; rather, the teacher helps students improve their present skills. Teachers who adopt the critical approach accept their own fallibility; they recognize that they do not know what a perfect, correct, or even adequate, skill would be. Moreover, even if they do know what a perfect skill is, teachers who adopt the critical approach recognize that they cannot transmit such knowledge, since students do not acquire knowledge from without. And even if teachers do present what they think is a perfect skill, and the student imitates or copies it perfectly, the student would actually be reproducing the teacher's skill: the teacher would have reproduced a replica of himself, of his way of doing things. Many teachers of skills, of course, do just this, paying no heed to Emerson's caustic criticism of such goings-on: "One of you is enough!" The real objection to such teaching, of course, is that it does not promote growth in the skill area. Even if the teacher were Ted Williams, or Julius Erving, or Ernest Hemingway, successful replication of their skills by students would neither enrich nor lead to further progress in sports or in literature.

This is why I suggest that teachers abjure goals and take up agendas instead—why their focus should be on helping students improve the skills they have, rather than trying to teach them new skills. Teachers and schools should never claim that they will teach students how to read, or how to write, or how to speak French, or how to perform any skill. The only logical, practical, and moral claim educators can make is that they will help students become better readers, better writers, better speakers of French, or better performers of some specific skill.

The coach, after pointing out the mistakes in the student's performance, may, of course, make suggestions about what the student should do, but these are suggestions, not descriptions of the "correct" way to perform the skill. The coach provides these suggestions to help the student in the process of trial-and-error elimination. These suggestions can reduce the number of trials the student must conduct in order to improve his or her performance.

As I see it, the primary role of the teacher is to be a critic—a role long ago proposed and carried out by Socrates. This is why I call this approach the critical approach. Yet many, especially those who are practicing teachers, object to the very notion that teachers should criticize student performances. These folks may sometimes cite both B. F. Skinner and Carl Rogers to prove that *good* teachers do not criticize; good teachers, they tell me, praise the students' performances and positively reinforce the students' behavior. These people have a point, a valid pedagogical point. And this brings me to the third aspect of an educative environment. So far, I have characterized an educative environment as a free environment—a place where students "feel free" to disclose their present level of proficiency; and, second, a critical or responsive environment—a place where students receive negative, or critical, feedback that helps them uncover inadequacies in their present level of proficiency (inadequacies of which they were unaware). The third aspect of an educative environment is that it should be supportive.

A Supportive Environment

In a supportive environment, students feel secure and confident, not threatened or anxious. Since criticism *is* threatening and anxiety-provoking for most of us, those people who object to teachers being critical have a point. Yet unless students do uncover the inadequacies in their performance, they will not improve. They will continue doing the same thing, performing in the same way. So the teacher must see to it that students receive critical feedback. Yet this criticism should take place in a supportive environment. This seems impossible.

It is possible, however, if the teacher keeps in mind the difference between the person and the performance. The teacher can support the student while criticizing the student's performance. In supporting the student, the teacher continually expresses confidence in the student's ability to improve, continually encourages and praises the student's capacity to do better. Moreover, to criticize the student's performance is the premier way teachers can show that they do care, that they do have what Carl Rogers calls unconditional positive regard for their students. If the teacher indiscriminately accepts and praises every performance of each student, this conveys the message that the teacher does not take the performance seriously and, therefore, does not really care about helping the student to improve. A supportive teacher, as I construe it, is a teacher who criticizes the student's performances but continually expresses sincere confidence in the student's ability to improve, whereas a teacher who kindly and warmly and tolerantly accepts and even praises every student performance is a teacher who expresses disregard for students, who cares nothing about helping them to improve their skills.

Teachers tell me that students must have self-confidence. I agree. But they, being teachers who have goals, link student self-confidence with level of performance or achievement. As they see it, students who best achieve the teacher's goals will have high self-confidence. This is probably so, but self-confidence that is based on one's performance or one's knowledge shades into self-righteousness, which prevents growth. Instead of rooting student self-confidence or self-esteem in performance or achievement, the teacher should root it in the student's ability to do better, to improve.

So, if teachers want to promote growth, they should:

Criticize the student's performance or knowledge; never criticize the student.
Praise the student; never praise the student's performance or knowledge.

Moreover, teachers who are concerned about the students' self-confidence and self-esteem are usually empathetic as well. But since they link self-confidence with level of performance or achievement, they try to set goals they believe the students will be able to attain and thereby gain self-confidence. This debilitates the schools by lowering the expectations of what students can do. These teachers lower the expectations of students not out of ignorance, nor prejudice, nor malice—they do it simply because they are teachers with goals, who have empathy for their students.

The answer is not to get teachers to have higher expectations, nor to have them raise their standards. Rather, teachers should abandon goals. Teachers should have no predetermined expected outcomes for students, no preset standards, no expected kinds of student performance. Instead of having a goal, teachers should adopt an agenda. Then, the teacher's task becomes one of helping students get better in some skill, or area, or domain. Teachers would then become concerned with improvement, not with correct performance. One felicitous outcome of abandoning goals is that teachers would no longer discriminate in favor of the "best and brightest" students. So long as teachers do have goals they will always look more kindly upon those students who attain those goals with the greatest celerity. But if teachers have no goals and are concerned only with helping students improve, they will regard *all* students equally, since from this perspective all students are equal: all students can always improve, continually.

So far I have talked about using the critical approach to teach skills. What about teaching understandings, which is the primary focus in the teaching of history, the sciences, and literature? How does the critical approach work in teaching understandings?

TEACHING UNDERSTANDINGS WITHOUT GOALS

The analysis presented so far about the origin and growth of skills holds, I think, for all other kinds of knowledge, including our understandings. That is, our understandings come from us; we are born with them, or we create them. And we create them through the procedure of trial-and-error elimination. Moreover, they are never perfect; we can always improve them.

"Understandings," as I use the term here, are possible only for human beings, since understandings are a product of speech and human language. An "understanding," as I construe it, is a theory embodied in language—in speech, or in writing, or in print. Without language, understanding cannot exist. When we say that a dog, or a cat, or a horse, or some other animal, "understands" a command or a request, we do not mean that the animal has a theory embodied in language, but only that it can and does respond to a given signal. The signal triggers or releases the expected behavior. This behavior is markedly different from the conduct of a child who understands the statement: "The ball is on the table." One may, of course, insist that the dog or horse does "understand." I do not, however, want to argue about the meaning of the word "understand." I simply want to point out the obvious difference between skills, or kinesic knowledge, and understandings, or objective knowledge. Kinesic knowledge is subjective knowledge; it is a part of the organism. Understandings, however, are objective knowledge because such knowledge is detached or detachable from a knowing subject: it is, or can be, placed "out there"—embodied in speech, or in writing, or in print.

Thus as I use the term, a child cannot understand until he or she begins to speak. An understanding is a theory—a conjectured hypothesis—embodied in language. And as Piaget has forcefully demonstrated, and as anyone who pays heed to small children can attest, a young child's understandings are always inadequate, always mistaken. Over time, those understandings improve, get better. This improvement takes place, as Piaget claims, in stages that follow an invariant order. At any rate, as the evolutionary epistemologists see it, our understandings improve, or get better, through the procedure of trial-and-error elimination: when we uncover errors in a (trial) understanding, we then modify that understanding by eliminating the error.

Since our understandings, like our skills, are theories or conjectures that we create, and since they, like skills, grow through trial-and-error elimination, it follows that teachers can use the critical approach here, too, in order to facilitate the growth of their students' understandings. Once again, teachers can do this by creating an educative environment: a free environment that elicits the students' present knowledge, a responsive environment that will provide critical feedback to that knowledge, and a supportive environment that will encourage students to modify their present knowledge. In this free environment, students will disclose what they know or understand; the critical feedback will help them uncover the inadequacies in their present understandings; and the support they receive will enable them to modify their understandings in light of the uncovered inadequacies.

In helping students to improve their present understandings, the teacher who uses the critical approach begins by presenting the subject matter, or portions of the subject matter, to the students. The subject matter—I am thinking here of history and the sciences—consists of the accepted understandings of experts in the fields, i.e., their conjectured theories. The teacher usually presents these conjectured theories of the experts in spoken language (e.g., a lecture), or in written or printed language (e.g., a text, or textbook). Here, the subject matter functions as "didactic material"—material that helps the students to improve their own understandings. Maria Montessori employed didactic materials in teaching small children. I am suggesting that teachers construe all texts and lectures as didactic materials. When so construed, the text (or lecture) does three things: it sets the agenda, it elicits the students' present understandings, and it provides critical feedback to the understandings that the students disclose.

When I say that the lecture, or the text, sets the agenda, I mean that it identifies what areas of the *students'* present knowledge are to be improved. The content of the text (or lecture)—what it is about—consists of some of the currently accepted understandings (conjectured theories) in the field of history, or the field of science. Students, at whatever age or educational level they may be, each already have their own understandings (conjectured theories) about these matters, even though their understandings may be vague, inchoate, unarticulated. The teacher's agenda is to help improve the students' understandings of the matters the experts have focused upon. Thus, teachers do not transmit the conjectured theories of the experts; rather they *present* them to the students via a lecture or a text.

In addition to setting the agenda, the lecture or text elicits the students' present understandings. This happens whenever anyone reads a text (or hears a lecture): such an experience educes one's *own* understandings of the matter under consideration by the author (or the lecturer). Since we all seek cognitive order, most of us usually assimilate what is presented in the text (or lecture) to our present knowledge, and what we cannot assimilate we reject or ignore. In this way, we maintain our cognitive equilibrium. Most of us further enhance our cognitive equilibrium by reading books, articles, and newspapers that present understandings like our own—material that will not cause us cognitive disequilibration, material that will strengthen our present understandings.

But teachers who use the critical approach do not want to strengthen the present understandings of their students; they want to improve them—by helping students uncover the errors in their present understandings. So they ask their students to concentrate on what they disagree with in the text (or the lecture), what the students think is wrong, mistaken, erroneous. That is, the critical teacher directly asks students to criticize the understandings (conjectured theories) presented by the author of the text (or by the lecture)—asks them to present arguments and counterexamples that will refute what was presented. The criticisms the students put forth will indirectly disclose their own present understandings, since the criticisms they raise must rest upon their own understandings.

In response to the criticisms students put forth, the teacher, or other students, try to come up with counterarguments to, or counterexamples against, those criticisms. Sometimes, these counterarguments will respond to the actual criticisms put forth and sometimes to the assumptions the criticisms rest upon. This creates a critical dialogue—not between the teacher and the student, but between the student and the text (or the lecture). The teacher serves only as the interlocutor—explaining, elaborating, defending, the understandings presented in the text (or the lecture). At times during the dialogue, the teacher may switch sides, elaborating and articulating as forcefully as possible a criticism presented by a student. The teacher's primary function is to keep the critical dialogue going, to keep it on target, and to keep it fair and honest. So the teacher acts as both interlocutor and referee.

In responding to the criticisms that students make, the teacher can sometimes simply refer to passages in the text (or the lecture) that refute the student's criticism. But often the teacher will have to go beyond the text (or the lecture) to refer to other understandings (conjectured theories) accepted in the field in order to produce counterarguments to the criticisms that students have put forth. Thus, in order to function as a critical teacher, one must know the subject matter field, must know its structure or logical coherence. Every field of knowledge has a structure, a coherence that logically excludes contrary understandings. Hence, one cannot make any claim that one wishes about the past, say, nor about the physical universe, not when such claims contradict the understandings accepted in the subject matter field.

This is not to say that the understandings that compromise the present state of a field will not change. The state of the field will change—through future criticisms that will reveal inadequacies it contains. No field is, or can be, perfect. Since we fallible human beings have created the theories that make up a given science or body of knowledge, none will ever comprise perfect descriptions that "fit" all the facts. Yet, at any given time, each body of knowledge, or science, has a more or less logical structure, which means that it can "kick back" when it is criticized.

Once again, the most powerful form of argument the critical teacher can employ in the classroom critical dialogue is the modus tollens:

$$
\begin{array}{ll}
(1) & p \supset q \\
(2) & \underline{\quad -q} \\
(3) & \quad -p
\end{array}
$$

Let p be the criticism proposed by the student. Let q be what is entailed by p; that is, $p \supset q$. The teacher points out that if what the student claims is true (p), then q follows: $p \supset q$. But then the teacher presents arguments to show that q is false: $-q$. Therefore, it follows that p is false: $-p$.

Let us suppose that the student has argued, or has assumed, that Christianity influenced the Stoic philosophy. Let this be p. The teacher then points out that this would entail the claim that Christianity antedated Stoicism: $p \supset q$. But q is false: Stoicism antedated Christianity: $-q$. Therefore, p is false: $-p$. It is not the case that Christianity influenced Stoicism.

The critical teacher's task is not to convince students that the text (or the lecture) contains truths, for the teacher is not out to get them to accept the understandings presented in the text (or lecture). Rather, the critical teacher *uses* the text (or lecture) to challenge, probe, and test the students' present understandings, uses the text (or lecture) to try to help students uncover some of the inadequacies in their present understandings.

Teachers who use the critical approach must see to it that students take seriously what is presented to them; the teachers must see to it that students critically encounter what is presented to them. This is not a matter of motivation, but instead a matter of ensnaring students into the procedures of a critical approach. Students have to present their own criticisms of the text (or lecture)—either orally or in writing. Furthermore, the teacher must take these student criticisms seriously: rephrasing them to be sure they are understood; perhaps reformulating them to make them as strong as possible; and then presenting, or educing from other students, counterarguments, or counterexamples, that will engender a critical dialogue.

A COMPARISON OF THE MODERN TEACHER AND THE CRITICAL TEACHER

Let me first briefly summarize the critical approach. It is based on evolutionary epistemology, which claims that we never receive knowledge, but rather create it; we create it by modifying the knowledge we already have; and we modify our existing knowledge only when we uncover inadequacies in it that we had not recognized heretofore. Accepting this as an explanation of how knowledge grows, I have suggested that teachers construe their roles as facilitators of the growth of their students' knowledge.

One way teachers can do this is to create educative environments—environments wherein the students can educate themselves, environments wherein students will improve their knowledge by modifying or refining their present knowledge through the procedure of trial-and-error elimination. An educative environment has three aspects: it must be *free,* so that students will voluntarily disclose their present knowledge; it must be *responsive,* so that students will receive critical feedback; and it must be *supportive,* so that students will try again when the critical feedback uncovers the inadequacies in their knowledge. The most important aspect in this approach to teaching is the critical feedback the student receives, which is why I have called this the critical approach to teaching.

The modern way of teaching, in contrast, consists of "transmitting" the correct understandings or skills to students. Here, the teacher is an authority: someone who possesses the correct understandings or skills—whether the skill be drawing, singing, dancing, writing, or whatever. The modern teacher's role is to show students the "correct" way to perform some skill, or to impart to them some correct understandings.

The Modern Teacher . . .	The Critical Teacher . . .
	. . . *first* presents models that:
demonstrate the correct performance.	elicit the students' present level of proficiency.
	. . . and, *second,* intervenes in order to:
correct the students' errors.	help students uncover errors in their performance.
	During this transaction, the teacher provides support that is:
contingent upon how well the students' performance approximates the "correct" performance.	not contingent upon the students' performance, but given unconditionally to the students themselves as agents capable of improvement.
	As a result of this transaction, the students:
modify (model) their present skills in imitation of the "correct" performance.	modify (improve) their present skills by eliminating the inadequacies uncovered.

Look first at how the modern teacher teaches skills. The teacher provides models or demonstrations of the correct performance—how to sing, dance, draw, or whatever the skill may be—which the students then copy or imitate until they attain the level of proficiency the teacher has predetermined to be correct. The chart above brings out the differences between the modern and the critical approaches.

Now let me compare the modern with the critical approach to the teaching of understandings. In both approaches, the teacher starts off by presenting some portion of the subject matter to the student by a lecture or a text. With the modern approach, the teacher may attempt to prepare or motivate the students to receive what is presented. After presenting the material, the teacher intervenes, but the intention is different with each approach. The modern teacher intervenes in order to "get the material across," to see to it that the students grasp it "correctly" and remember it. The teacher does this by answering students' questions, by asking the students questions, by suggesting how the material that was presented relates to something else, or by suggesting how useful the material is and asking the students to make their own applications of the material presented. The aim here is to have the students internalize, or make "their own," the understandings the teacher has presented.

With the critical approach, there is no need to prepare or motivate students to *receive* the material, since they will not receive it; they will encounter it, critically. After presenting it, the teacher intervenes to elicit student criticism of the material and then provides critical dialogue—between the students and the material presented (see the chart below). The intent here is to use the presented material to help the students improve their present knowledge.

Before further discussion of the modern and critical approaches to teaching skills and understandings, I want to make clear that the modern approach does not, cannot, work—at least not as intended. For although modern teachers believe that they are transmitting skills or understandings to students, they, like the teachers who use the critical approach, are actually creating an educative environment wherein students educate themselves by modifying their present knowledge through the procedure of trial-and-error elimination. The difference between the two environments is that the one created by the modern teacher is much

The Modern Teacher . . .	**The Critical Teacher . . .**
. . . presents material that:	
the student is to learn.	the student is to encounter.
. . . and then intervenes in order to:	
get the material across and help students accept and remember the material.	elicit the students' criticisms of what is presented and provide critical feedback to the students' criticisms in order to create a critical dialogue.
If this transaction is successful, the students:	
accept the material presented and make it their own.	improve their present knowledge.

more controlled. The modern teacher so completely controls the environment that in the matter of skills, every trial performance a student makes that does not approximate the performance that the teacher has predetermined as "correct" is ruled an "error"; while in the matter of understandings, any understanding the student has that does not approximate the understanding that the teacher has predetermined as "correct" is ruled a "mistake." In this kind of environment, the student becomes disposed to look upon the teacher as the authority for what is correct.

With the critical approach, the teacher is not an authority, but rather a critic, someone who can help the students uncover mistakes, errors, inadequacies, in their performances and in their understandings.

In the matter of teaching understandings, the authoritarianism of the modern approach is more pronounced, since here the teacher ignores the students' present understandings. As a result, the educational transaction does not get the student to modify or change his or her own understandings, but simply to create another set of understandings—understandings to satisfy the teacher or understandings to pass the test. Such understandings do not usually "take"; they do not become part of the students' own knowledge and usually disappear after the test.

With the critical approach, however, the students' own understandings undergo change.

By focusing on the students' own knowledge, the critical approach helps students improve *that* knowledge. The subject matter becomes the vehicle that helps students do this. Thus, with the critical approach, "real learning" occurs because this approach is more in accord with the trial-and-error process through which growth takes place.

MOTIVATION, STUDENT RESISTANCE, AND SEQUENCING

The critical approach not only better accords with how knowledge grows; it also overcomes or eliminates some of the persistent problems connected to the modern approach to teaching.

One of these is the problem of motivation. Because they do not seek to get the students to learn some predetermined knowledge, do not try to get students to receive and accept what they present, teachers who use the critical approach eliminate the problem of motivation. Since there is no substantive knowledge that the critical teacher wants students to learn, there is no necessity to motivate them. In the critical classroom, the concern is to help students improve their present knowledge. Students will do this when they uncover inadequacies in their present knowledge—because they, like all organisms, have a built-in aversion to disequilibration, and when they uncover inadequacies in what they had thought was adequate knowledge, they experience disequilibration. If the environment is sufficiently supportive, this disequilibration will not make them anxious or angry, but instead will lead them to modify (improve) their present knowledge.

Another problem that teachers who employ the modern approach often encounter is student resistance. Students fail to learn, or refuse to learn, or complain about learning. The critical approach eliminates this problem because, once again, teachers who use this approach are not imposing knowledge on students, neither forcing, nor coercing, nor cajoling them, to learn. It may, of course, happen that students may resist criticism, may refuse to recognize that their knowledge is inadequate. When this happens, the teacher should not press the matter, but, rather, resolve to create an environment more supportive for that student, so that criticism will become less threatening.

One other problem that the critical approach avoids that bedevils the modern teacher is the matter of ordering and sequencing the subject matter. Because the modern approach assumes that students receive knowledge from without, modern teachers construe the growth of knowledge as the accumulation of correct understandings, or the correct sequencing of skills. So for the modern teacher of skills and understandings, the choice of the starting point in education becomes decisively important. Thus, modern teachers of reading and writing worry about whether to teach from the bottom up (first letters, then words, then sentences, then paragraphs) or from the top down (begin with the text as a whole and attend to parts only in context). Modern teachers must take care that students do not fall into error at the very start. Indeed, some modern teachers have expressed the desire to turn their students upside down so as to dump out all the erroneous knowledge they have in their heads, this would allow the teachers to install a more firm foundation on which to construct a correct edifice of knowledge. Some teachers, those who are more student-centered, the so-called progressive teachers, also worry about the correct starting point. But they identify it with the students' needs, their purposes, their experiences, their problems. By beginning with the students' interests or needs, they say, the teacher will provide a solid foundation for the growth of knowledge.

In addition to starting with a solid foundation—whether it be the "basics" of a subject matter or the students' interests and needs—modern teachers pay close attention to the sequence of the material presented. They follow such guidelines as from the simple to the complex, from the concrete to the abstract. This proper sequencing, they say, helps students more readily grasp what the teacher presents to them.

With the critical approach, however, the teacher recognizes that no subject matter rests upon a solid foundation. Knowledge is not an edifice in need of a foundation; rather, it is more like an organ, or an organism, adapted to the environment. Like organs or organisms, knowledge is conjectural. Since there are no foundations, there is no problem of finding the correct starting point, no problem of following the correct sequence. The growth of knowledge, like the evolution of organs and organisms, takes place through trial-and-error elimination. The evolution or growth that occurs depends upon the inadequacies uncovered. With the critical approach one can begin any place in teaching skills or understandings, so long as what is presented leads to a critical approach to the students' present knowledge, so long as the student uncovers some of the inadequacies in his or her present knowledge and eliminates or reduces them. Once again, the critical teacher has no goals, only an agenda: to help improve certain skills or certain understandings. The teacher cannot initially know what understandings or levels of proficiency the students already possess. These must be elicited and then criticized. Since the teacher cannot know beforehand what the criticisms will focus on, there can be no planned sequence for promoting the growth of the students' knowledge.

THE CRITICAL APPROACH AND CONTINUAL GROWTH

Yet, make no mistake about it, the modern approach to teaching both skills and understandings is effective, often dramatically effective.* I have already suggested that the modern approach is effective insofar as it accords with the dynamics of growth, i.e., trial-and-error elimination. However, as Howard Gardner's study of Chinese education makes clear, the modern approach does not facilitate continual growth. First of all, in the matter of skills, the performance goals set by the modern teacher place a ceiling on the growth of the students' skills. Some, exceptional, students may transcend these goals, but most students will not, since the modern teaching approach leaves students with the conviction that they have attained mastery—of writing, or drawing, or singing, or whatever the skill may be—when they have achieved the predetermined performance goals. In the matter of understandings, the modern approach does not encourage continual growth either, insofar as students believe that they have achieved the "correct" understanding of the matter at hand when they have attained that understanding predetermined by the teacher.

A second reason why the modern approach hinders continual growth is that it does not encourage self-criticism in students. As I have repeatedly pointed out, criticism is the key or trigger to growth. This means that students must become critical of their own performances and their own understandings—while remaining confident in their ability to "do better"—if they are to

*See, for example, Howard Gardner's *To Open Minds: Chinese Clues to the Dilemma of Contemporary Education* (New York: Basic Books, 1989) for an account of how the modern approach as practiced by Chinese educators can promote high levels of performance in large numbers of students.

continue growing. But instead of encouraging them to be self-critical and seeking more growth, the modern approach to teaching encourages students to look to authorities in order to confirm or justify that their performance is correct or that their understandings are right. Authoritarianism always stifles growth.

The antidote to authoritarianism is fallibilism—the acceptance of human fallibility. If human beings accept their fallibility, then they will realize that they can never have perfect knowledge. And this means that there can be no correct models of skills that students should imitate, no right understandings that students should grasp. Thus, teachers—if they accept their human fallibility—can never "correct" a student's performance of a skill, nor tell a student that he or she understands some matter correctly.

Here some defenders of the modern approach may argue that there *are* correct ways to do some things, that there are correct understandings of some factual matters, and that teachers must teach students what is correct: teachers must teach students the correct way to add, subtract, and multiply; the correct way to spell; the correct way to pronounce words; and so on. Moreover, they must teach students the correct understandings of the past (George Washington was the first president of the United States) and the correct understandings of the universe we inhabit (the planets revolve around the sun in elliptical orbits).

My answer is that, yes, teachers can and should present our current skills and our current understandings to the students, but not as being the *correct* skills, the correct understandings. The histories of mathematics, spelling, and speech, as well as the history of science, all reveal that our current ways of doing things and our current understandings have all evolved over time, and continue to evolve in the same way all evolution takes place: through trial-and-error elimination. Thus, our current skills are not perfect, nor are our understandings, either. They are inadequate and erroneous, even though we cannot presently ascertain those inadequacies or errors. They cannot be perfect since we fallible human beings created them.

Thus, when critical teachers present our current skills and current understandings to students, the teachers do not want the students to accept this knowledge and make it their own. Rather, critical teachers present this current knowledge to students as "didactic material," as material that will help students improve their own knowledge.

PROGRESSIVE TEACHERS

Now that I have contrasted the critical approach with the modern approach, I want to compare it with the progressive approach to teaching. As I understand it, the progressive approach starts not with the presentation of material, nor with the demonstration of a skill, but, rather, with a problem for the student to explore. The teacher who uses the critical approach can also employ this strategy, since posing problems for students is an excellent way to elicit their present knowledge.

Progressive educators, however, are not concerned with eliciting students' present knowledge. Instead, they want students to *discover* new understandings or skills.

When the progressive educator intervenes, it is not to help students uncover inadequacies as in the case with the critical approach, nor to correct their mistakes, as with the modern approach. Rather, the teacher who adopts the progressive approach intervenes in order to give students help, guidance, hints, that will help them discover a solution to the posed problem.

Progressive educators do support their students, although this support is linked to the solutions students come up with to the problems they encounter. Some progressive educators praise students only when they come up with the correct solutions, while other progressive educators accept and praise whatever solution the students come up with to the problem at hand.

Although advocates of progressive education claim it is radically different from the modern approach to teaching, from the angle of vision of the critical approach, both the modern and the progressive are the same, insofar as both assume that knowledge comes from outside the knower.

Those who use the progressive approach worry about "real" learning; they want the knowledge that the student acquires to

The Progressive Teacher . . .	The Critical Teacher . . .
. . . presents problems to students in order to:	
encourage students to explore.	elicit students' present knowledge.
. . . and then intervenes in order to:	
give students guidance, suggestions, hints, to help them discover solutions to the problems presented.	help students uncover errors and inadequacies in their present knowledge.
During the transaction, the teacher provides support to the students:	
by praising the solutions they come up with.	unconditionally, as agents capable of improvement.
If the transaction is successful, the students:	
discover knowledge.	improve their present knowledge.

"take." The key, they tell us, is to have students discover knowledge rather than try to transmit it to them. Knowledge that the students themselves discover is knowledge that they will retain, the argument goes. To help them discover this knowledge, the teacher must present students with problems that are meaningful, relevant, and significant. Meaningful problems are those related to the students' past experiences; relevant ones are those related to their present experiences; and significant problems are related to their anticipated future experiences. To come up with problems that students will find meaningful, relevant, and significant, and that, at the same time, will lead students to discover that knowledge that teachers have predetermined to be important for students to know, is a tall order, indeed. And, in truth, many progressive educators—e.g., Carl Rogers—have abandoned having the teacher predetermine what knowledge the students should discuss. According to Rogers, when teachers give students freedom to learn—i.e., freedom to discover—real learning will take place: the knowledge will "take."

If my earlier analysis of the growth of knowledge is correct, then "real" learning, knowledge that "takes," is the result of the modification or refinement of the knowledge one already has.

We do not receive knowledge from without, and this means that we do not, cannot, discover knowledge. So in spite of what progressive educators claim to be doing, they, like all teachers, are actually creating an environment wherein students improve their own knowledge via the process of trial-and-error elimination. According to my interpretation, the problems that the progressive educator presents to students function to elicit their present knowledge and also help them uncover some of its inadequacies. This leads students to modify their present knowledge, not to discover new knowledge. As always, the process is one of trial-and-error elimination. The important question is: Does the progressive approach facilitate this process? Presenting problems to students can, as we saw, facilitate trial-and-error elimination. But the crux of an educative environment, as pointed out earlier, is that it provides critical feedback that helps students uncover errors in their present knowledge. On the face of it, the progressive approach does provide feedback to students, at least that approach Dewey set forth does. Dewey insisted that we learn by performing experiments.* As he saw it, learning will take place when students subject their proposed solutions to experimentation. Experiment will confirm, or disconfirm, the solution. The assumption here is that knowledge that is confirmed,

*In the progressive classroom environment set forth by Carl Rogers, teachers have little or no concern with experimentation as part of the education transaction. Indeed, the Rogerian classroom is so unstructured that it provides students little or no negative feedback. As a result, in such an environment, as many have complained, students simply mess about—their knowledge does not grow. It is true that the knowledge of the best and the brightest students may grow in such an environment, but this is not because of anything the teacher does; rather, it is because the best and brightest already have a propensity to engage in trial-and-error elimination activity, even in the absence of a structured classroom environment. This is what makes them the best and brightest. The defenders of the Rogerian approach complain that structured environments actually hold back the better students. This probably does happen sometimes. But such an occurrence does not mean that a Rogerian approach is better for such students than a critical approach. It simply means that the critical feedback provided to them in the critical approach must be individualized. Actually, of course, the critical approach *is* individualized since teacher intervention is always directed at the particular mistakes each student makes.

shown to be true, will take, and it will more readily take if students confirm it through experiments they actually conduct.

Here we can see that the feedback provided in the progressive classroom is positive feedback—a validation or confirmation of the student's knowledge. Although experiments can and do provide negative (critical) feedback to students, progressive educators favor experiments that "work," experiments that confirm the proposed solution by providing positive feedback and thus strengthen belief in that solution. Yet seeing to it that knowledge "takes" is only part of the teacher's task. Teachers must see to it that a student's knowledge will continue to grow. By creating environments wherein students seemingly discover knowledge and where they perform experiments that confirm that knowledge, the progressive educator strengthens the student's belief in that knowledge; but this does not facilitate continual growth; in fact, it actually hinders it.

This accusation will come as a surprise to progressive educators since one of their oft-repeated claims is that students in their classrooms learn how to learn. They say that we learn by solving problems and that their students learn how to solve problems. Here they follow Dewey, who announced that humans have advanced beyond the trial-and-error method all other organisms use to solve problems. Humans, he maintained, have developed the scientific method, the method of experimentation. In accord with this, progressive educators want schools to become laboratories, and students embryonic scientists. In the progressive classroom, they conclude, not only do students discover knowledge, but also they learn how to learn—i.e., how to solve problems by the scientific method.

The claims of the progressive educators are wrong. In spite of Dewey's claims, humans have *not* advanced beyond the trial-and-error approach to solving problems used by other organisms. From the amoeba to Einstein, knowledge grows in the same way. The difference between Einstein and the amoeba, however, is that whereas the amoeba dislikes to err, Einstein is intrigued by it: he consciously searches for his errors in order to eliminate them, which improves or advances his knowledge.

Einstein is critical, but the amoeba cannot be critical because it cannot *face* its knowledge; it is a part of it. "Only objective knowledge is criticizable," Popper points out. "Subjective knowledge becomes criticizable only when it becomes objective, and it becomes objective only when we say what we think; and even more, when we write it down, or print it."*

Karl Popper has also shown that scientists do not perform experiments in order to solve problems, but, rather, they perform them to test any and all proposed solutions to a problem. A solution that passes the test is not, however, confirmed. Our "successful" experiments merely demonstrate that so far we have not found out what's wrong with the solution. Therefore, in spite of what progressive educators believe, we do not know how to solve problems; we do not possess a method for solving problems. We have only a way for weeding out false and inadequate solutions: the critical approach—experimentation is but one form of criticism.

If knowledge does grow through trial-and-error elimination, then attempts to justify knowledge, to strengthen commitment to it—as the progressive educators attempt to do—will actually hinder or curtail the growth of knowledge. Nevertheless, the notion that teachers should insist that students accept only justified knowledge is deeply implanted in educational thought. In my next section, I will try to uproot it.

*Karl Popper, *Objective Knowledge* (Oxford: Oxford University Press, 1972), p. 25.

PART TWO

AGAINST POSTMODERNISM

4

Knowledge without Justification

Teachers who have goals almost always have a justificatory theory of rationality. According to this theory, rationality consists of accepting only that knowledge which is justified as true. Since teachers with goals want their students to accept the knowledge the teachers present, they usually try to justify what they present by "proving" it is true: they employ "experiments," "evidence," "arguments," and "testimonials" to convince the students that this knowledge is true.

More than this, teachers with goals try to get students to subscribe to this theory of justificatory rationality. "How do you know?" these teachers frequently ask their students. By posing this question, they piously purport to be teaching students to be rational, i.e., teaching them to accept only statements that they can justify and to reject all they cannot justify. To be rational, the teachers insist, is to accept only justified statements, i.e., statements that can be shown as true.

Yet justification is impossible.

Many teachers painfully learn this when sharpshooter students turn the tables on them and begin asking the teacher: "How do *you* know?" No matter what answer one gives to justify a statement or claim, the questioner can follow up with "How do you know?" Likewise with any answer given to *that* question. And so on into infinity. Attempts to justify knowledge can lead to an infinite regress. It is logically impossible to justify knowledge.*

The only way to escape from this infinite regress is to abandon that theory of rationality that insists we accept only statements that can be justified. This, actually, is what most modern teachers do. They shut off the infinite regress by appealing to some ultimate authority, such as "expert testimony" ("All scholars in the field agree that this statement is true!"), or "scientific experiment" ("Tests have proven that this statement is true!"), or "sensory experience" ("If you look carefully, you will see that this statement is true!"), or "power" ("I'm the teacher, and I say it's true!").

When teachers do this, they set up some authority as infallible. Through this strategem, they escape the infinite regress, but only by accepting a statement or claim that is itself not justified. So in escaping from the infinite regress, they contradict the theory of rationality that says we should accept only statements that are justified: their claim that the final authority is authoritative is not itself a justified claim. But more than this, appeals to an ultimate (unjustified) authority convert education into an authoritarian transaction. That is, students must accept the statement as true because some authority (whatever it may be) says that it is true. Now, much can be said against authoritarianism in education; the most important criticism, however, is that authoritarianism prevents the growth of knowledge. Any knowledge justified by an infallible authority cannot be criticized, hence, cannot be improved.

Yet not all teachers succumb to authoritarianism. In recent years, some—those I will call postmodern teachers—have taken a different route to justification, a route charted by a movement in philosophy that tries to justify knowledge while avoiding infinite regress and contradiction.

*Note, too, that teachers of skills cannot justify the skills that they teach are correct. All such attempts to justify skills as correct are guilty of the logical fallacy of affirming the consequent. (See pages 24 and 25.)

In the second half of the twentieth century most philosophers came to recognize that knowledge—by which they meant what they call propositional knowledge and what I have called "understandings" or "theories," i.e., knowledge encoded in language—can never be justified as true, at least in any absolute sense. In the fifties, many philosophers began to follow the later work of Wittgenstein, abandoning the ideal of truth and replacing it with the quest for meaning. Meaningful knowledge, they said, was useful knowledge; i.e., the meaning of a symbol, a word, a phrase, a statement, a text, was now said to depend upon the way language is used. And since different groups use language differently, or play different language games, the meaning of a proposition becomes relative to a speech community. Although they abandoned the notion of truth and substituted meaning in its place, these philosophers still retained the belief that knowledge had to be justified. But now justified knowledge was simply knowledge that had meaning to some group. A justified proposition was one used in accordance with the language rules of some linguistic community. To justify a proposition, one had only to describe its meaning to some group. The proposition was not, of course, justified as true, but it was justified as certain. Here's how Wittgenstein put it in one of his books:

> 445. But if I say "I have two hands," what can I add to indicate reliability? At the most that the circumstances are the ordinary ones.
>
> 446. But why *am* I so certain that this is my hand? Doesn't the whole language-game rest on this kind of certainty?
>
> Or: isn't this 'certainty' already presupposed in the language-game? Namely, by virtue of the fact that one is not playing the game, or is playing it wrong, if one does not recognize objects with certainty?
>
> 447. Compare with this $12 \times 12 = 144$. Here, too, we don't say "perhaps." For, in so far as this proposition rests on our not miscounting or miscalculating and on our senses not deceiving us as we calculate, both propositions, the arithmetical one and the physical one, are on the same level.
>
> I want to say: The physical game is just as certain as the arithmetical. But this can be misunderstood. My remark is a logical and not a psychological one.

> 448. I want to say: If one doesn't marvel at the fact that the propositions of arithmetic (e.g., the multiplication tables) are 'absolutely certain,' then why should one be astonished that the proposition "This is my hand" is so equally?*

The foundation for certainty is the language game itself, the system of language uses of a linguistic community. Thus, justification occurs within a system (a linguistic community). There can be no rational justification of the system itself. Rather, as Normal Malcolm, one of Wittgenstein's disciples, put it: "We are taught, or we absorb, the systems within which we raise doubts. . . . We grow into a framework. We don't question it. We accept it trustingly. But this acceptance is not a consequence of reflection."†

This philosophic approach to justification resulted in the compartmentalization of knowledge: each language community became a more or less closed circle, incommensurable with all others. As Wittgenstein wrote, the statement "We are sure of it" does not mean that just every single person is certain of it, but that we belong to a community which is bound together by science and education.‡ Accordingly, then a proposition meaningful to a biologist may not be meaningful to a historian, or may have a different meaning. Justified knowledge is relative to each community of discourse. But if this is so, then justified knowledge must be relative in time as well as space, so that not only do biologists have justified understandings of the world *different* from the justified understandings accepted by historians, but biologists of the nineteenth century had justified understandings *different* from those justified understandings of biologists of the twentieth century. They belong to *different* communities of discourse, so the meanings of terms and propositions are relative to each community.

This new, or postmodern, approach to the justification of knowledge has appeared in the field of sociology as well as in

*Ludwig Wittgenstein, *On Certainty* (New York: Harper and Row, 1972), p. 58.
†Quoted in William W. Bartley III, *Unfathomed Knowledge, Unmeasured Wealth* (LaSalle, Ill.: Open Court, 1990), p. 235.
‡Wittgenstein, *On Certainty*, #298, p. 38.

philosophy, especially in the sociology of knowledge. In their highly influential book, *The Social Construction of Reality,* Peter Berger and Thomas Luckman popularized the notion that societies, or groups, create or construct reality—their knowledge of reality, which is, they say, all the reality there is: there is no reality beyond human artifice. As with Wittgenstein's language games, sociology of knowledge makes all knowledge relative.

This postmodern approach to justification appeared in other academic fields as well. Thomas Kuhn, who did much to popularize it in the field of history of science, employed the term "paradigm" to explain how the scientific knowledge of the past could be different from and incommensurable with that of the present. According to Kuhn, scientists understand the universe only in terms of the reigning paradigm of their era. A new paradigm replaces an older one in the scientific community when too many anomalies appear with the latter. Accordingly, the justified understandings of present scientists are no better than those of the past—only different.

Epistemological relativism is the heart of postmodernism. For if one abandons the search for true knowledge and replaces it with the search for meaningful knowledge, then—since meanings *do* vary among different speech communities—knowledge *is* relative. But if all knowledge is relative, then there can be no such thing as the growth of knowledge. This is the conclusion postmodernism leads to, a conclusion subscribed to by postmodern teachers of the humanities and the social sciences and even by some teachers of the natural sciences.* Thus, postmodern teachers do not, *cannot,* construe education as the growth of knowledge. Instead of promoting the growth of their students' knowledge, postmodern teachers acculture them to the language

*Thomas Kuhn denies that he is a relativist, since he does think that there are criteria, such as accuracy of prediction, number of problems solved, simplicity, and compatibility with other speculation, that can be used to establish that some scientific theories are better than others. But these are pragmatic criteria that have nothing to do with the truth of the theories. "There is," he says, "no theory or independent way to reconstruct phrases like 'really there'; the notion of a match between the ontology of a theory and its 'real' counterpart in nature now seems to me illusive in principle" [*The Structure of Scientific Revolutions,* 2d ed., enlarged (Chicago: University of Chicago Press, 1970), p. 206].

games of one or more academic fields. They teach students how the experts in each academic community use language. Here is how Neil Postman and Charles Weingartner put it:

> To begin with, we are in a position to understand that almost all of what we customarily call "knowledge" is language. Which means that the key to understanding a "subject" is to understand its language. In fact, that is a rather awkward way of saying it, since it implies that there is such a thing as a "subject" which contains "language." It is more accurate to say that what we call a subject *is* its language. A "discipline" is a way of knowing, and whatever is known is inseparable from the symbols (mostly words) in which the knowledge is codified. What is biology (for example) other than words? If all the words that biologists use were subtracted from the language, there would be no "biology." Unless and until new words were invented. Then, we would have a "new" biology. What is "history" other than words? Or astronomy? Or physics? If you do not know the meaning of "history words" or "astronomy words," you do not know history or astronomy.*

Why should students *accept* acculturation into the language games of the experts? Especially if that language game has nothing to do with truth? The only answer that postmodern teachers can give is that we are all continually playing games—the teacher plays the game of teaching, the student plays the game of studenting, and the experts play the games of biology, history, or whatever the subject is. The teacher's game is to socialize or acculturate students to the language games of the experts. The students' game consists of learning those language games of the experts. Q.E.D.

Here, as with much of postmodern thought, description substitutes for explanation: take it or leave it. At bottom then, education in the hands of postmodern teachers becomes a political activity. That is, those who have the power impose language games on those who do not. This is what education is.

Some postmodern teachers (or are they post-postmodernists?) have come up with an alternative approach to education. Instead of simply acculturating students to some linguistic

*Postman and Weingartner, *Teaching as a Subversive Activity* (New York: Delacorte Press, 1969), p. 102.

community, these educators set out to expose how various groups—especially, white, male Europeans—have established and maintain oppressive control over other groups—specifically, blacks, females, and non-Europeans—by socializing them to the language games of the oppressors, or to the constructions of reality the oppressors have created. These post-postmodernist educators want to unmask the traditional school subjects of history, literature, social sciences, and even the natural sciences. These post-postmodern teachers help students to "see through" the traditional subject matters, help them see how the "oppressors" have used these subject matters, both to oppress females, blacks, and non-Europeans and to get them to accept this oppression and victimization by telling students that the knowledge taught to them is justified. This post-postmodern approach to education makes students conscious that education is nothing but a political act, a transaction that socializes people to some linguistic community. Moreover, through this approach, students are brought to understand that the program of traditional subject matters—created by the hegemonic linguistic community of white, male Europeans—must be destroyed and a new one set up in its place—one that is feminist, black, and non-European: an educational program that will empower those who heretofore have been victimized.

In this highly abbreviated history of knowledge in the last half of the twentieth century, I have tried to show the consequences of the attempt to justify knowledge. First, the recognition that it is impossible to justify knowledge without appeal to some (unjustified) final authority led the postmoderns to abandon the pursuit of true knowledge and replace it with the quest for meaningful knowledge. When they substituted meaning for truth, "justified" knowledge became "certain knowledge," that is, knowledge contained in statements commonly used by some linguistic community. Thus, a given statement was justified knowledge if it had meaning for some group. This renders all knowledge relative.

Teachers who subscribe to the postmodernists' conception of justified knowledge construe education as a transaction in which students acquire justified knowledge, which means that the teachers acculturate their students to the language games of the experts in the various subject matter fields.

A final group of teachers—those whom I have labeled post-postmodern teachers—have taken on the task of laying bare what the postmoderns uncovered. They have concluded that any attempt to teach anyone any knowledge whatsoever is a political act of imposition. In consequence, the post-postmoderns see their role as that of making students conscious of how education oppresses blacks, women, and non-Europeans by imposing on them the language games of white, male Europeans. They encourage students to actively resist all attempts to educate (oppress) them.

As I see these developments, both postmodern educators and post-postmodern educators have corrupted education, corrupted it far beyond the sorry state modern educators had brought it to. At the root of this debacle is the quest for justified knowledge. The modern educators correctly believed that the growth of knowledge is conceivable only if truth exists as an ideal—growth consists in getting closer to that ideal. They thought that we could approach truth by building upon a "solid knowledge base," a foundation of knowledge *justified* as true. But as the critics of modern education correctly maintained, we cannot justify knowledge as true; we can only justify it as meaningful. However, when postmodern educators abandoned truth and replaced it with meaning, they made the growth of knowledge impossible. For if, as the postmodernists claimed, justified knowledge is knowledge that has meaning to some linguistic community, then knowledge is relativized and the growth of knowledge simply cannot take place.

The way out of this debacle is to give up all attempts to justify knowledge—but to retain the ideal of truth. This is the solution proposed by Karl Popper.

According to Karl Popper's evolutionary epistemology, all of our knowledge, both our skills and our understandings, are conjectural: knowledge consists of conjectures that we make. And although we cannot demonstrate that our knowledge is true or adequate, we can, via criticism, uncover its inadequacies or falsity. By uncovering falsities and inadequacies in our knowledge and eliminating them, our knowledge grows. It moves closer to truth. We can demonstrate this by showing that our latest conjectures are better than our earlier conjectures insofar as the latest ones do not contain the errors the earlier ones did. Of course, our latest conjectures cannot be perfect, since we are fallible,* and, in time, we will, via criticism, uncover and eliminate the errors these conjectures contain. So the progress and growth of knowledge is not only possible; it is endless—endless because our ignorance is infinite.

The critical approach to knowledge that Popper proposes is nonjustificationist. This is perhaps the most misunderstood aspect of Karl Popper's evolutionary epistemology. For most philosophers, including the postmodern philosophers—indeed, for most people—knowledge, real knowledge, is knowledge that is justified—verified, confirmed, validated, or certain. Popper, however, maintains that knowledge cannot be justified as true. Here he agrees with the postmodernists. He even agrees with the postmoderns that knowledge can be justified as meaningful by reference to some linguistic community. But this, he says, is of no significance since it throws no light on the important question of the growth of knowledge; indeed, concern with meaning casts this question into darkness and obscurity by making knowledge relative to a linguistic community.

For Popper, all knowledge is conjectural and always remains so. Yet although we cannot ever justify it as true, we need not abandon truth as a regulative ideal. Instead, he says, we should abandon certainty. He clearly distinguishes truth from certainty: truth, or true knowledge, is objective—it corresponds to the facts; it is a description that fits the facts. Certainty, on the other hand, is rarely objective; it is usually no more than a strong feeling of conviction or trust. In abandoning justification, we give up certainty about our knowledge. But we do not give up truth. (In contrast, the postmodernists give up truth and retain certainty as an ideal.) Here is what Popper says: "Thus, although I hold that more often than not we fail to find the truth, and do not know

*Note that this is not proposed as a *true* claim, but as a conjecture. There is no way to justify the claim that human beings are fallible. The conjecture that we are fallible can be refuted by uncovering an infallible human being.

even when we have found it, I retain the classical idea of absolute or objective truth as a regulative idea; that is to say, as a *standard of which we may fall short*."*

What Popper has done is to replace justificatory rationalism with critical rationalism. For Popper, criticism becomes the alternative to justification. When we criticize theories or understandings, we attempt to show that they are *not* true. Thus, we are always searching for true knowledge, even though we can never give reasons to show that we have found true knowledge. Popper replaces justification: providing valid reasons (positive reasons) for the truth of a theory, with criticism: providing valid reasons (critical reasons) against its being true.

Moreover, from Popper's perspective, knowledge is no longer compartmentalized, no longer enclosed in the closed circle of a linguistic community. Rather, there is a unity of knowledge, since in all fields knowledge grows and improves in the same way—through the evolutionary approach of trial-and-error elimination.

Some may suspect that critical rationalism will result in skepticism. This is not so, however, since critical rationalism does allow us to regard one theory or understanding as preferable to another. This consists in pointing out that, and how, one theory has hitherto withstood criticism better than another. The critical reasons do not justify a theory, for the fact that one theory has withstood criticism better than a second theory is no reason for supposing that the first theory is actually true. But although critical reasons can never justify a theory, they can be used to defend (but not to justify) our preference for it. Our critical reasons are conjectures, and so we should be ready to give up a preferred theory should new critical reasons speak up against it, or at least be ready to renew the critical discussion. Here, we must be clear that criticisms are never conclusive. They cannot be since they are always conjectural, and thus open to counter-criticism. One can continue the critical dialogue indefinitely. Yet there is no infinite regress here since there is no question of prov-

*Karl Popper, *Realism and the Aim of Science* (Totowa, N.J.: Rowman and Littlefield, 1983), p. 26.

ing, or justifying, or establishing, anything. It is the demand for proof or justification that generates an infinite regress and creates a need for an ultimate termination of the discussion. This is the heart of the difference between justification and criticism.

In urging teachers to adopt what I have called the critical approach, I am asking them to give up justificatory rationalism for critical rationalism. The critical teacher recognizes that no knowledge can be justified—not the students' present knowledge, nor the knowledge of the experts that the teacher presents to the students. All knowledge is conjectural. So when teachers who adopt the critical approach present the theories of the experts, they present them as imperfect conjectures of fallible human beings, conjectures that students should encounter critically. Students do not accept, nor assimilate, the knowledge that the teacher presents; rather, they use it to promote the growth of their own knowledge—via critical dialogue.

In the classroom of a critical teacher, "How do you know?" questions do not arise. Instead of asking students to justify their knowledge, the critical teacher creates an environment in which their knowledge can grow—an educative environment where students can disclose their knowledge, receive critical feedback to it, and then modify it in light of the inadequacies uncovered.

5

Against Socialization

It has become commonplace to construe education as a process of socialization. This was not always the case. Indeed, such a construction of education came into being only with the early proposals for the education of the masses, which first arose in the late sixteenth century. Until that time, there had been no need to educate those who grew and prepared the food or those who made and prepared the artifacts necessary to maintain society. Ever since the time of the ancient Greeks, education had been reserved for the leisured few, the leaders of society. Their education consisted of an initiation into their cultural heritage. They studied the classic texts of western culture, texts that initiated them into the beliefs, ideas, values, understandings, and attitudes that would guide their conduct in running the world.

The aftermath of both the Protestant Reformation and the rise of the modern state during the sixteenth and seventeenth centuries brought the religious and political authorities to the realization that the masses now had to be educated—educated so that they would embrace the *correct* religious doctrines and be loyal to the *correct* political authorities. The education of the masses was quite different from that education provided for the leaders of society. For the masses, there would be no initiation into the cultural tradition. They were simply to be socialized—to be transformed into loyal subjects and pious believers. The ends, the goals, the outcomes of such an "education" were preset, predetermined.

During the next two centuries, first the churches, and then the states throughout the western world, began to provide such an "education" for the masses. Over this time, the construction of education as a process of socialization took root and by the twentieth century had become commonplace throughout western civilization.

What I have called "modern education" is an education that is actually based on the notion that education is socialization. I have so far spoken only about the matter of intellectual socialization, where teachers attempt to socialize students intellectually, to get them to accept and subscribe to predetermined theories, ideas, and understandings. But the notion that education is socialization encompasses more than this. It includes socializing the students to the arrangements of the society—the political, social, and economic arrangements. Thus, modern education has always been a process of preparing students to accept and subscribe to the existing policies, practices, and procedures in the existing society—a process of molding, shaping, transforming children to fit into what is: the existing society, the existing polity, and the existing economic system.

Such a construction of education is authoritarian. Yet it was not recognized as such so long as those who provided it, as well as those who received it, believed that the existing social, political, and economic arrangements were proper, correct . . . just. As long as they so believed, everyone viewed the socialization of the young as a beneficent and humane transaction; education, or socialization, as they saw it, prepared people to live the kind of lives they *ought* to live.

Although there was earlier sporadic criticism of the attempt to use the schools to deliberately socialize the young to the existing society, a full-blown resistance to this kind of education came only with the arrival of what I call the postmodern educators. And the criticism of education came about only after these educators first became aware of the unfairness and injustice in the existing society itself. Elsewhere I have argued that television in the 1960s helped raise the consciousness of people, especially young people, about the unfair relationships in America between the races, between ethnic groups, between classes, and between men and women.* By the 1970s, more and more people were complaining that American society was controlled and run by white, male Anglo-Saxons and that all the existing political, social, and economic arrangements served their interests. Once people became aware of these unfair and unjust relationships, it became clear to many educators (the postmoderns) that the schools served as agencies to legitimize the existing society, as agencies that prepared the young to accept and fit into these arrangements. As the postmoderns saw it, the schools socialized the young to an immoral society.

Instead of abandoning socialization, the postmoderns simply altered its goals. In the hands of the postmodern educators, the schools continued to socialize the young, but to socialize them differently. Thus, there emerged feminist education, Afro-centric education, bilingual education, and education for the handicapped—each program purportedly intended to empower heretofore oppressed students; but actually each program shaped and molded them in some predetermined way—socialized them, not to the existing arrangements, but to some not yet existing "ideal" arrangements.

The argument against construing education as socialization—whether of the modern or postmodern kind—is that it ignores human fallibility. Those who attempt to socialize students presume to know what a good society is: the moderns assume that the existing society is good; the postmoderns assume that the society of their dreams is good. The assumption that they know what a good society is supposedly gives them a warrant to socialize the young to that society. But no fallible human being can have such wisdom. No one of us knows what a good society is. A second argument against construing education as socialization is that it denies agency to students. It imposes a predetermined set of values, beliefs, attitudes, and behaviors on them.

*See "Epilogue," *The Imperfect Panacea: American Faith in Education* (New York: McGraw-Hill, 1990, 3d ed.).

Finally, such a conception of education does not facilitate growth—of the society, of the polity, or of the economic arrangements. If the modern teachers do succeed in socializing students, this simply strengthens and perpetuates the status quo. And if the postmodern teachers do succeed in their socialization projects, this simply strengthens and perpetuates a new status quo.

Throughout this book, I have argued that the Darwinian theory of evolution provides a theory for the growth of knowledge, and that this evolutionary epistemology supplies a basis for teachers to facilitate the growth of their students' knowledge. Here, I want to suggest that the Darwinian theory of evolution also provides a theory for the growth of culture, and supplies a basis for teachers to facilitate that growth.

Human beings not only create knowledge; we also create our culture—our political, social, and economic arrangements. And just as the knowledge we fallible humans create is always inadequate, so also are our societies, polities, and economic systems inadequate. No matter how carefully we design them, no matter how well-intentioned we may be, the social, political, and economic policies we formulate, the processes we develop, and the practices we create will all have unanticipated consequences—some of which will harm some people. But like our knowledge, our cultures can get better. Just as we can reduce the errors in our knowledge and thereby improve it, so also can we diminish or reduce the inadequacies and insufficiencies in our political, social, and economic arrangements. In both our knowledge and our culture, improvement takes place through the procedure of trial-and-error elimination. The culture we create is always a kind of trial. We improve it by uncovering the inadequacies it contains and eliminating them. And we do this by being critical.

Here, then, is the task for teachers who want to improve the culture: educate students to be critical—critical citizens, critical consumers, critical workers, and critical members of whatever groups they belong to. I am not suggesting that schools turn out graduates who will tear down the society and destroy it. No, what I envision are schools producing concerned critics, people ready to take on the task of the continual renewal of the culture, prepared to engage in the critical dialogue through which the procedure of cultural trial-and-error elimination takes place.

Instead of trying to socialize the young to accept and give thanks for the existing social, political, and economic arrangements, critical teachers will encourage them to criticize those arrangements, as well as to criticize all proposed alternatives to the existing arrangements. These criticisms will be met by countercriticisms from the teacher, or from other students in the class, creating a critical dialogue. A critical dialogue, as I understand it, is an engagement in which the participants try to uncover the weaknesses, inadequacies, errors, in their own ideas and theories. A critical dialogue is not a debate where one tries to prove that one's ideas are correct. Nor is it a fight where one tries to demonstrate that the ideas of one's opponents are wrong. No, a critical dialogue is a procedure of trial-and-error elimination, an engagement wherein one tries out one's own theories and ideas in order to uncover their inadequacies. When the agenda or focus of a critical dialogue is about the (existing or proposed alternative) political, or economic, or social arrangements, then the outcome is an improvement of the participants' understandings of the arrangements, an improved understanding of their strengths and weaknesses. Above all, participation in a critical dialogue produces in people an openness to continued dialogue about those arrangements.

A critical teacher should be neither the defender of the arrangements that exist nor the advocate of any change or modification in those arrangements. Here, the school is a critical agency, *the* critical agency of the society, a place where all criticisms can be voiced and every criticism met with countercriticism. Such an education prepares people to live in an open society—a society where all arrangements are open to continuous criticism.

I fear that to many, such a conception of society may sound idealistic—an academician's version of how society ought to function. Yet I submit that what I propose is not unlike the way our society already *does* function, in a rough and ready way. Indeed, *all* cultures evolve via this procedure of trial-and-error elimination. But throughout human history, error elimination has usually taken a violent and bloody course, frequently requiring fights, battles, wars, and revolutions. The genius of our culture lies in our having devised institutions that permit and facilitate *peaceful* modification of inadequate and unwanted policies, practices, and procedures. Our political, social, and economic arrangements have evolved, and continue to evolve, through peaceful trial-and-error elimination because we tend to regard these arrangements as trials, trials that we can change or modify when public criticism reveals inadequacies. No more dramatic example exists of this than the changes made during the last half century in the relations between the races and the relations between men and women. In the course of changing those relationships, there was violence in some cases, to be sure, especially with regard to changes in the relations between the races. But considering the scope and depth of the changes effected, they came about peacefully for the most part. The changes came about as the result of criticisms made of the then existing policies, practices, and procedures that governed racial and gender relations. The elimination of some of those uncovered inadequacies has improved our society. Our culture has evolved.

Not only do we use trial-and-error elimination to improve our culture, but we have also devised institutions to facilitate peaceful cultural evolution. In the realm of biological evolution, nature is the mechanism that selects and eliminates the unfit, but in the case of cultural evolution, we have created institutions to do this job. In the economic sphere, for example, we have grievance committees, unions, and the mechanism of collective bargaining to uncover and reveal unfair management policies and practices; we also have consumer groups, environmental groups, and regulating agencies to uncover inadequate and evil practices of business and industry; and there are regulatory boards that monitor labor practices, too. In addition, the market itself serves as a selection institution that facilitates economic growth by eliminating goods and services that are inadequate or that are too costly. In the social sphere, we have created civilian complaint boards, ombudsmen, advocacy groups, civil rights commissions, public hearings, and voluntary rights groups of many kinds to uncover unfair and discriminatory practices. It is in the political realm that we have most fully developed institutions that facilitate growth or improvement. Our political institutions, like the Constitution, the Bill of Rights, the separation of powers, checks and balances, frequent elections, and judicial review, all function to help us uncover harmful, bad, and inadequate laws, policies, practices, and procedures.

All these institutions that help us uncover inadequacies in our social, political, and economic arrangements are like fortresses that protect us against harm. But fortresses by themselves cannot protect us; they must be manned. So also with our institutions: they must be manned by people who know how to use them. This is where education comes in. Critical teachers prepare concerned critics to man these institutions.*

This was the reasoning behind Thomas Jefferson's "Bill for the More General Diffusion of Knowledge" in Virginia in 1779. In the preamble to that bill, he wrote: ". . . it is believed that the most effectual means of preventing this [tyranny] would be to illuminate, as far as practicable, the minds of the people at large, and more especially, to give them knowledge of those facts which history exhibiteth, that possessed thereby of the experience of other ages and countries, they may be enabled to know ambition under all its shapes, and prompt to exert their natural powers to defeat its purposes. . . ."

With the critical approach I am proposing, the history taught to students will inform them how the political, social, and economic institutions described above came into being; what they are supposed to accomplish; and how they function and operate.

*Here I may seem to be going against my proposal that teachers should have no goals and should not socialize students. Is not educating students to be critical a form of socialization? Does not such an endeavor commit teachers to a goal? I think not. For there is no substantive goal inherent in educating students to be critical. There is no socialization. One never knows where criticism may lead; there is no telling where students will wind up, or what answers they will come up with. Teaching people to be critical does not entail teaching them any value, belief, theory, or behavior. Nor does it mean that students so taught will have no beliefs, values, or theories. It simply means that they will hold lightly those they do have, hold them tentatively—open to criticisms and ready to abandon them should criticism uncover their inadequacies.

Students thus educated will be able to man those institutions and keep them in repair, since no institution can be perfect. As Thomas Jefferson said about the political institutions designed to help people protect themselves: ". . . it appeareth that however certain forms of government are better calculated than others to protect individuals in the free exercise of their natural rights, and are at the same time themselves better guarded against degeneracy, yet experience hath shown, that even under the best forms, those entrusted with power have, in time, and by slow operations, perverted it to tyranny."

Moreover, students educated by the critical approach I have described in this book will be critical; they will know how to engage in critical dialogue. And, above all, they will accept human fallibility, so that they will recognize that our cultural arrangements will always be imperfect, but understand that those arrangements can continually be improved in peaceful ways—through critical dialogue.

Each of us belongs to many groups: we are male or female, black or white, old or young, rich or poor, workers or employers, urbanites or suburbanites, etc. At any time, we may discover that some policy or practice or procedure in the existing society harms or victimizes one of the groups we belong to. It behooves all of us, therefore, to see to it that everyone is educated to become a concerned critic, able to use, and, if necessary, to repair, the institutions set up to uncover and eliminate that which harms us or others. If we do not educate people to be concerned critics, we are paving the way for those who are victimized to resort to violence and bloodshed to secure relief.

The critical approach I recommend to replace the socialization approach to education will not bring about total change in the society, nor will it likely bring about radical change. Instead, the changes will be piecemeal and gradual. The focus is always on the removal of concrete evils in the existing arrangements, not the construction of ideal, or even good, arrangements. A critical approach to our culture, conducted by concerned critics, can create not a perfect culture, but simply a better one.

PART THREE

BEYOND POSTMODERNISM

6

Education without Essentials

Most commentators on contemporary education in America see the curriculum as the problem, and many are the debates about what subjects the schools should teach. This is understandable since this concern follows logically from the assumption that knowledge comes to us from without. This assumption indicates that education is a process of transmitting knowledge to students and that the *only* educational problem is: . . . What shall we transmit to them?" . . . But in this book I have argued that human beings are not receptors of knowledge, nor discoverers, either: knowledge does not come to us from without. We are the creators of our knowledge.

From this angle of vision, I view education as a transaction to promote the evolution or growth of knowledge. This evolution takes place, as does all evolution, through the procedures of trial-and-error elimination. In all cases of biological evolution, nature eliminates unfit organisms; in the evolution of knowledge, natural selection is replaced by critical selection, and criticism eliminates the errors contained in our conjectures. So I have suggested that rather than try to transmit knowledge to students, teachers should create an educative environment, an environment that is free, responsive, and supportive, and that will facilitate the growth of students' knowledge. In this environment, the teachers do not transmit subject matter; they present it to students. The subject matter becomes what I call (following Maria Montessori) "didactic material." That is, the subject matter establishes an agenda, elicits the students' present knowledge, and provides critical feedback to the students' knowledge.

It is at this point that we confront the matter of the curriculum. What subject matter should the teacher present to the students? Critical teachers want to facilitate the growth of the students' knowledge, but what knowledge should they facilitate? What is worth knowing?

Throughout history, the matter of the curriculum has been treated as a philosophical question, and those who have discussed it have assumed that there is essential knowledge, knowledge that everyone should have. Aristotle, for example, thought that education consisted of liberal studies, those studies that liberated, those studies through which one realized oneself as a human being. These were studies that cultivated the intellect, the highest part of a human being. Plato, Aristotle's teacher, thought that it is the nature of the society, not the nature of man, that determined what the essential educational subjects are. That is, he thought that students should learn whatever is necessary to maintain the existing society. Since different people usually have different roles to play in any society, this means that there will be some degree of differentiation in what students study, depending upon their probable destinies in the society.

In America, ever since the creation of the public schools, the question "What's worth knowing?" has been treated as a political problem rather than a philosophical one. That is, those who control the schools have decided what is worth knowing. At the outset, those who controlled the schools were white males, usually of western European ancestry. They imposed their views of what is worth knowing on the rest of the people. In time, however, control over the schools became more democratized, as parents, educators, and students secured a voice in determining what's worth knowing. In consequence, school curricula became more varied as new programs and new courses of study appeared beside the traditional fare. In the second half of the twentieth century, largely as a result of the criticisms leveled by those I have called postmoderns, various groups within the society—blacks, women, non-English-speaking, and the disabled—began to demand and secure courses of study to suit the needs of their groups. In consequence, during this period the public school curriculum further expanded through the introduction of women's studies, Afro-centric studies, education for the handicapped, and bilingual education.

The programs offered in the public schools have grown, but this growth has been one of accretion rather than evolution. More courses and more functions have been added to those that already existed. This expansion is directly traceable to the attempt to treat the question "What's worth knowing?" as a political matter. As the control over the schools became increasingly democratized, the logic of democratic decision making inexorably led to the expansion of the public school curriculum.

Here's how it happened. As I argued earlier, the democratic institutions we have created do serve as selection devices for eliminating inadequate laws and policies. But these institutions were set up to screen out those laws and policies that violate recognized rights. They were not created to serve as mechanisms to decide how to distribute or allocate goods, such as education. When our democratic institutions are made to serve this purpose, the result is an expansion of the functions of the school and an expanded curriculum.

First, minority groups, those who had little or no control over the public schools, resorted to the courts to complain that the existing public school curriculum discriminated against them. In a democratic society, the courts act to protect the rights of all citizens. The relief sought and gained by these minority groups came in the form of new educational programs and courses of study specifically designed for them. Thus, the curriculum and the functions of the school expanded.

Second, legislators in democratic polities—whether these be local school boards, state assemblies, or the federal Congress—who seek reelection must satisfy the demands made by their constituencies, and so they pass legislation that caters to special-interest groups. These special-interest groups lobby for a wide variety of courses of study: environmental education, sex education, driver education, drug education, consumer education, health education, safety education, multicultural education, to mention only those programs most commonly sought after by special groups. The democratically constituted legislative bodies adopt laws and policies that provide funds and set up programs for the education of all public school students in these many and varied matters.

As the curriculum has expanded and schools try to teach so many different courses of study, they end up not teaching any of them well. The overexpanded public schools have become more and more ineffectual. And at the same time, of course, the costs of public education have risen to pay for all the expanded offerings and the specialists needed to teach them. We now spend approximately 33 percent more in real terms per capita on students in elementary and secondary schools than we did ten years ago, but most measurement studies show a decrease in learning.

What is to be done?

The ineffectiveness of the schools and the rising costs to maintain them have become a national crisis. Yet we cannot go back to the kind of nondemocratic control of the schools that existed in the nineteenth century. Nor can we reform the schools through democratic control, since all such efforts lead to more expansion of the curriculum.

How can we decide what the schools should teach? How can we decide what's worth knowing? Clearly, no one person—no matter how wise he or she may be—can decide what everyone else should know. Nor should any group—no matter how large it may be—impose its answer on the rest. The only way to decide this question seems to be to allow people themselves to choose what is worth knowing, and in the case of young children, to allow their parents to choose. Such an approach may be possible within the public school system of a local district as is being done in District Four in New York City, or throughout an entire state, as is being done in Minnesota. Or such an approach may move beyond public education to include private schools through some sort of voucher or scholarship provisions. Or such an approach may be carried out through the complete privatization of schools. In any event, making the answer to the question "What's worth knowing?" a matter of public choice converts the question into an economic one. Instead of being decided through democratic politics, it will be decided by the market.*

If each school provided its own program, its own course of study, and parents could choose which one to send their children to, the competition in the market among the schools for clients would weed out that knowledge that is *not* worth knowing. Thus, the market would promote the evolution of the curriculum through the procedure of trial-and-error elimination.

Yet if we were to have a marketplace of schools, each with a different curriculum and course of study, would not this endanger the society? As Hirsch and Adler, and others, have argued, our society, any society, needs a common curriculum to provide a bond among people—a set of commonly held beliefs, ideas, understandings, values, and attitudes.† Without such social bonds, will not the society become factionalized and end up in anarchy?

This argument must be heeded. Yet although I agree that there must be a bond that holds people together in a society, I am not convinced that such a bond must consist of substantive knowledge taught by schools. This was true of the age of tribalism, but it is no longer possible, nor desirable, in our free, pluralist society. Our society is increasingly an abstract one. Unlike a tribal society, we have little or no face-to-face contact with most of the members of our society. And even with those we do—say, fellow pedestrians on the street or fellow riders on the subway train—we have, as a rule, no personal relation with them. In such a society, we do not share—or do not know . . . or care, if

*The market approach to schooling is well explained in Myron Lieberman, *Privatization and Educational Choice* (New York: St. Martin's Press, 1989), and John Chubb and Terry Moe, *Politics, Markets and America's Schools* (Washington, D.C.: The Brookings Institution, 1990).

†E. D. Hirsch, *Cultural Literacy* (Boston: Houghton Mifflin, 1987); M. Adler, *The Paideia Proposal* (New York: McGraw-Hill, 1982).

we do share—the same substantive beliefs, understandings, theories, and values. So I suspect that in this pluralist society, we cannot agree on what's worth knowing. Nor *should* we agree if we want to preserve our free, pluralist society.

Yet we can agree, and I suspect most of us *do* agree, on how whatever is taught ought to be taught—or better, we agree on how it ought not be taught. That is, no one wants schools to indoctrinate students, to propagandize them, to impose knowledge on them. No one wants this to be done, and yet most teachers do not know how to avoid doing this.

The approach I have presented in this book, the critical approach, does provide an approach that is not impositional, not indoctrination, not propaganda. With the critical approach, all understandings and skills are exposed to maximum criticism in order to eliminate as much error and inadequacy as possible. In this book, I have focused on what is the most salient feature of the critical approach: the role of the teacher in the educational transaction. I have talked about the classroom environment. But if the critical approach is to make any headway, it must be institutionalized in all the arrangements of the schools. We must pay attention to the entire school environment. Today, all of the schools' arrangements—I am thinking of such matters as examinations, textbooks, grading, educational technology, and classroom management—are founded under and function within notions and assumptions I have rejected: assumptions and notions that knowledge comes to us from without, that teachers should have goals and should pay heed to student purposes in order to "transmit" to them knowledge that is "justified."

The refinement and modification of these other aspects of schooling in order to bring them into line with the critical approach will take time and ingenuity. Yet such transformations are *not* necessary preconditions for teachers to convert their classrooms into educative environments. Most teachers can begin to employ the critical approach tomorrow.

It is this critical approach that I suggest will create a social bond within the society. Instead of possessing shared bits and pieces of knowledge, people who are taught this way will have a common outlook toward all knowledge. They will recognize and accept human fallibility and thereby realize that all knowledge is conjectural—never final, never complete—but continually improvable, through criticism, through the uncovering and elimination of errors. They not only will be ready to hold all received and new knowledge open to criticism, but will be prepared and able to participate in the critical conversation through which knowledge and culture grows and evolves.

PART FOUR

CRITIQUES AND REBUTTAL

7

Critical Pedagogy and the Realities of Teaching

Peter W. Airasian
Boston College

Professor Perkinson has written a challenging and provocative piece. He confronts his reader with propositions about education that are too often unexamined or taken for granted and turns the reader's perspective upside down regarding the role of educational commonplaces such as goals, purposes, and teaching. Unfortunately, the piece also is enigmatic, in that its brevity denies the reader both the elaboration and the examples that could clarify the argument.

As I understand them, the main precepts of critical pedagogy are as follows. (1) Since students must create their own knowledge, the aim of education cannot be to transmit knowledge to students (that is impossible) but to help them create and develop their own knowledge. (2) Knowledge itself consists of theories, hypotheses, and conjectures about phenomena that each student possesses at some level of sophistication. (3) Learning occurs when the student modifies his or her existing knowledge through trial-and-error recognition and the elimination of inadequacies in that knowledge. (4) The teacher's role is to help students modify their knowledge by creating a free, responsive, supporting environment in which students will disclose their present knowledge, receive critical feedback about it from the teacher, and modify it to accommodate the critical feedback.

Although there is much to discuss in Professor Perkinson's piece, I shall confine my comments to two areas—a few relatively brief observations and questions that arose when I studied the piece, and a more detailed examination of the role of the teacher in critical pedagogy. I approach my task from the perspective of a long-time observer of the realities of classrooms and teachers' lives therein. My comments are predicated on the expectation that education will continue to be group-based and that critical pedagogy will have to operate in a context in which teachers will interact with more than a single student at a time, although the interactions need not take place in the ways and settings presently employed.

GENERAL OBSERVATIONS

There are four issues in critical pedagogy that I should like to have explicated more fully: the role of educational goals, the basis for student motivation, the bounds of goalless teaching, and the nature of affective knowledge. In most of what follows, my remarks on these issues are less critiques than questions to be answered.

Educational Goals

Professor Perkinson argues that in critical pedagogy teachers have no goals for their students save modification of the students' existing knowledge; there are no ends except for the continual evolution of existing knowledge structures. It would seem, however, that an important and appropriate goal of critical pedagogy is student self-sufficiency in applying its values and processes. Given its trial-and-error nature, one can never know where the critical process ultimately may lead, but one at least would like to know whether the process of critical examination and knowledge modification is being applied by students. Self-sufficiency in this case need not imply perfection or an end to knowledge evolution, but it would seem that some degree of mastery of the critical *process* itself is necessary if the student is to apply critical strategies in the absence of teachers. While this outcome of teaching is not a substantive goal linked to subject matter proficiency, it does seem to be an important one for teachers of critical pedagogy. If it were not important, then growth would stop when teaching ended, and the vision of the critical adult would not be fulfilled. At issue here is the nature of goals (substantive versus process, ultimate versus intermediate) and the possibility and desirability of their attainment in critical pedagogy.

There are, of course, benefits to goals. They can help define some target point in a process, even though that point does not necessarily represent the ultimate or even a highly refined status. At least, they can provide a standard for both teachers and students to use in self-assessment. Self-assessment, or a sense of how one is doing, is not an inconsequential consideration given the uncertainty and indeterminacy of the educational process. Moreover, whether wisely or not, one can be certain that such goals will be demanded and carefully examined by parents in their efforts to assess the quality and success of the education their children are receiving. Goals need not be the minute, specific, reductionist statements that clutter present textbooks and that help foster the notion that the teacher's task is the transmission of small bits of specific information. The goals need not even be group-oriented. But their existence could provide some benchmark against which teachers and students could assess their progress—a benchmark both teachers and students will want and seek. It may be that some of the difficulties with goals in critical pedagogy, though certainly not all, could be overcome if, instead of talking about the finality of "a student attaining a goal," we talked about "the student developing or improving his or her knowledge."

In this regard, one also might question the extent to which goalless teaching is possible. In critical pedagogy, the teacher's central tasks are to present to students an agenda consisting of material they are to encounter, permit students to expose the current status of their knowledge relevant to the material, and help them see inadequacies in this knowledge. But to accomplish these tasks, the teacher must make decisions. Before presenting material, for instance, the teacher must first decide which materials to present and how to present them. Any material to be used will not contain within itself directions for how it should be presented to students. Moreover, before identifying inadequacies in student knowledge, the teacher must first decide what criteria to use in determining the adequacy of a student's knowledge. Thus, it seems likely that a teacher's answer to the question "Why did you decide to use these particular materials, methods, and criteria instead of other available ones?" will be based in part on implicit goals or preferences that the teacher has about what the students can do and about what they ought to be learning.

Student Motivation

Critical pedagogy rests heavily on the proposition that humans possess an inborn expectation of order. This expectation is argued to be the stimulus that motivates students to revise their existing knowledge in response to the identification of its inadequacies. This proposition requires more explication. It is a far journey from justifying an inborn expectation of order in terms of humans' cringing at thunder or being startled by lightning (page 12) to using it as a cornerstone in the theory of critical teaching.

Professor Perkinson argues that teachers do not have to motivate students to receive material because in critical pedagogy the material is encountered, not received. This may be so, but teachers still will have to motivate students to encounter the material. It is, I believe, naive to assume that all students will be motivated, interested, and cooperative in the process of the critical assessment and evolution of their knowledge. Motivation, interest, and other affective responses cannot be so simply relied upon in critical or any other kind of teaching.

Transmitting Knowledge

Are there situations in critical pedagogy in which a teacher might want to transmit information to students? I am thinking here of two circumstances that are not addressed directly in Professor Perkinson's piece but that raise the issue of information transmission as opposed to knowledge creation or modification. One situation occurs when rules for safety or social order are necessary to carry on an educational encounter, situations such as those that occur in a chemistry laboratory, industrial arts class, or reading group. Does one want students to observe laboratory safety rules or rules of social intercourse regardless of whether they have made these part of their personal knowledge structures? A second situation involves transmitting factual material such as addition facts, state capitals, chemical formulas, or sight reading vocabulary which students acquire for a variety of reasons but which, compared with knowledge as defined in critical pedagogy, are relatively discrete and isolated pieces of information. Such facts generally are nonconjectural and unlikely to change much in a student's lifetime; yet they can be important prerequisites for the evolution of students' knowledge structures. Is critical pedagogy the best way to facilitate students' acquisition of such information, and how would such a process work? Answers to these questions would more clearly lay out the domain and dimensions of critical pedagogy.

Affective Knowledge

Critical pedagogy is based on the argument that knowledge and skills do not come to students from without, but rather from within, from the student's own creation or modification of existing knowledge. Different students will formulate their knowledge and skill structures differently because each student must do it for himself or herself. Can the same be said for affective characteristics like the student's sense of interest, motivation, support, encouragement, and freedom, all of which are key to the success of critical pedagogy? If, like knowledge and skills, student affects cannot be transmitted but must be created or constructed by each student, what are the implications for a critical pedagogy that depends so heavily upon the student's perceptions of the affective features of the learning environment (e.g., free, supportive, noncensorious) or upon the student's willingness to encounter material and motivation to alter his or her knowledge? If affective characteristics are knowledge in the same sense as cognitive knowledge, then each student will construct his or her own particular knowledge or theory about what a free, supportive, noncensorious, interesting learning environment is. If this is the case, it is more appropriate to talk about unique affective environments perceived by each student than about affective environments in general. The multiplicity of such constructions and the need for the teacher to identify each student's particular one will complicate instruction greatly. If affective knowledge has different roots than cognitive knowledge, what are they? If affective knowledge has the same roots as cognitive knowledge, how could that influence the process of critical pedagogy?

The preceding four issues were not the only ones that arose from study of Professor Perkinson's piece. They were, however, ones that particularly piqued my interest, since they have practical implications for efforts to describe and implement critical pedagogy. I turn now to a more in-depth look at critical pedagogy as considered in the context of the realities of teaching.

TEACHING AND CLASSROOM REALITIES

Prescriptions for educational change, such as critical pedagogy, have to be examined in the reality of the context into which they will be placed. To this end, consider some realities of classrooms.*

*P. W. Airasian, *Classroom Assessment* (New York: McGraw-Hill, 1991).

First, classrooms are social as well as academic settings. A class is more than a group of students who happen to be in the same place at the same time; it is a society made up of people who can communicate with each other, pursue common activities, and follow rules of order. The classroom also is a place characterized by fast-paced, transitory activities that often call for immediate, practical, situation-specific teacher responses. It is a place where order is necessary and where teachers must know and attend to both the social/personal and academic characteristics and needs of their students. In many classroom interactions and transactions, it is difficult to separate these two dimensions.

Furthermore, the classroom is a place of isolation, both for students, who for most of their day are expected to work and act as if there were no other students around them, and for teachers, who have little daily interaction with colleagues. Teacher isolation is compounded by lack of clearly defined educational consequences and bases on which to judge success. It is difficult for teachers to identify the successes of their teaching because student achievement does not often manifest itself in immediate or obvious ways, nor in ways that can be directly related to teacher actions. In the face of this environment, teachers—and I believe students also—want and need some goals, standards, or criteria against which to assess the success of their activities.

Moreover, teaching itself is a normative activity; it is value-based and value-driven. All teachers operate with a general set of beliefs that they use to make sense of their world and to direct their actions in it. For the most part, these beliefs are tacit and include conceptions about the nature of intelligence, the factors that motivate students, the most desirable areas of student achievement, the conditions that foster learning, and the like. Such beliefs are based on personal experience, are used to defend teaching practice, are grounded in simple explanations and practical solutions, and are influential on teachers' classroom thoughts and behaviors. In a nutshell, these are the realities of teaching and classrooms within which critical pedagogy will be examined.

In addition, for teachers to succeed in critical pedagogic endeavors, they must assume many responsibilities and engage in many actions. According to Professor Perkinson, the critical teacher should create an environment where students feel free to disclose their present level of proficiency; construct an accepting, nonjudgmental, noncensorious, nonteaching environment; praise initial student efforts; help students recognize mistakes and inadequacies in their performance; get students to recognize the consequences of what they are actually doing; help students improve present skills; accept their own fallibility and recognize that they don't know what perfect performance is; keep in mind the difference between the person and the performance when criticizing the student's performance; have no predetermined expected outcomes for students, no preset standards, no expected kinds of student performance; serve as interlocutor and referee during discussion, explaining, elaborating, defending in a fair and honest manner; know both the structure and logic of a subject field to go beyond the text or lecture to produce counterarguments to student criticism; and ensnare students into the critical approach.

It is obvious from this list, and Professor Perkinson also emphasizes the point, that the teacher is the most important element in critical pedagogy. Substantial responsibility is placed on the teacher, which gives rise to two questions related to teachers' roles in critical pedagogy.

1. *Does the present context of teaching permit teachers to satisfy their defined responsibilities?* If the scenario of teaching and the classroom environment I have presented is even partially accurate, there will be serious impediments to the application of critical pedagogy. In the first place, teachers will have a difficult time separating the personal and academic sides of their students. In order to structure and maintain the social and academic aspects of the classroom society, teachers must know and understand their students in many different ways. For example, it is known that, in the first week or so of school, teachers form very detailed perceptions of their students' characteristics—both academic and personal—and use these perceptions to form expectations of students. It is also known that these initial perceptions and expectations remain relatively unchanged through the school year. First impressions count a lot. In this regard, teachers are no different from the rest of us, in that we all form impressions and expec-

tations of others, even in the most informal and transient social situations. How much more must teachers do this when faced with the reality of managing, interacting, and teaching students one to six hours per day? Further, teachers obviously have a vested concern in the success of their teaching and in their students' achievement. They are not dispassionate observers, either of their students or of classroom activities and transactions.

For these reasons, it is unrealistic to expect teachers to be nonjudgmental about their students or to have no predetermined expectations, outcomes, or standards for them. It also is unlikely that teachers can easily separate the student, the student's performance, and the context in which teaching takes place when criticizing disclosed knowledge. Teacher perceptions and expectations will influence the tone of the learning environment, so that free and supportive environments may be difficult to establish for every student.

Moreover, classroom isolation, lack of clearly identifiable student attainments, and contradictory standards for judging students' accomplishments conspire to encourage teachers to engage in self-assessment activities to answer the question "How am I doing?" As Professor Perkinson points out, the intent in traditional pedagogy is to determine how much of a set of predetermined facts, skills, and understandings students possess after being instructed; in most schools and classrooms, assessment is goal-based. The educational system reinforces the goal-based view through its textbooks, teacher preparation courses, and external mandates for specified student outcomes. Teachers accept this view and use students' test and worksheet performance to self-assess their own efforts. Parents and concerned adults reinforce this view by assessing the progress of both their children and the educational system in terms of goal-based, objective testing instruments. We are in a time when many people place more trust in the results of a 30-minute multiple-choice test than in a teacher's judgment based upon months of living with a child in the classroom.

Yet critical pedagogy does raise some interesting dilemmas for assessment. If there are no goals in the educational process, traditional goal-based assessments will be neither appropriate nor informative, although as just noted, they likely will be demanded by many publics for many reasons. If one cannot identify in advance either general or specific goals to be attained, assessment of students and teachers becomes a problem.

If it were possible to approximate, goalless assessment would be the logical outcome of critical pedagogy. Such assessment probably would have to rely much more heavily on descriptions and examples of individual students' performances than on group-administered tests. These descriptions and examples would be most pertinent to showing improvement in knowledge over time. What is presently called "authentic assessment," with its emphasis on descriptive, performance-based, non-multiple-choice assessment approaches, would seem to fit closely with the general tenor of critical pedagogy. However, it would be more difficult to gather evidence of this kind than to continue reliance on group, goal-based, objective tests; yet it could be done.

Certainly there is a place in educational transactions for activities that have no explicit student achievement goals—activities that the teacher selects because he or she believes they are worthwhile and educational, even though the precise experience and learning the student is to take away from the activity cannot be stated. It is not always necessary for purpose to precede activity. In fact, teachers often assess their own effectiveness in terms of the energy and interest with which students respond to teaching activities. Involvement is a necessary, but not sufficient, condition for knowledge growth. Yet there remains the need and public demand for assessment of more than student involvement.

The danger with any descriptive, nonjudgmental evidence of student involvement or performance is the inevitable pressure to make it normative and comparative, so that it can be used to rank and differentiate students. While teachers may be satisfied to know that a student was actively engaged in classroom activities or that the student's knowledge has evolved over time, others inevitably will want to know "by how much," "who was most involved or improved," and "what grade does this much involvement or improvement deserve?" Thus, given the social nature of classrooms and teaching, the teacher's need for self-assessment, and the internal and external demands for goal-based accountability, it will be difficult to establish the goalless, nonjudgmental, accepting, performance-focused environment needed for critical pedagogy.

2. *Are teachers in general or the educational profession itself up to the challenge posed by critical pedagogy?* The extent to which teachers presently possess or can be helped to acquire the values, attitudes, and critical skills needed to carry out critical pedagogy is a second question that must be addressed. It is easy to say that teachers must accept their own fallibility, create an accepting, nonjudgmental environment where students feel free to disclose, help students recognize their mistakes, ensnare students into the critical approach, and know both the structure and logic of a subject field. It is more difficult to make it happen.

Special knowledge and insight are required of teachers who will carry out critical pedagogy. They must work without goals. They must create environments in which students feel sufficiently secure to reveal their knowledge. They must be supportive, nonjudgmental, and nonexpectational. They must serve as interlocutor and referee during discussion. They must provide the critical reactions that will lead students to revise their existing knowledge.

It is not reasonable to assume that all or even most teachers now possess these capabilities. One reason for making this assumption is because it is not clear what exactly is necessary to create a "free, supportive, nonjudgmental" environment, although whatever is necessary probably varies from teacher to teacher, from student to student, and for each unique combination of teacher and student. How would one know when one had such an environment? Educational psychology and sociology offer some general guidelines, but little more. Experience is an important teacher, but is biased by the particular experiences one has encountered. If one who asks this question from the perspective of critical pedagogy itself would want to know how classroom conditions could be arranged so that students would ensnare themselves in the educational process and create their own perceptions of a free, supportive, nonjudgmental environment. It is clear that this question cannot be answered for all or even most students.

More to the point, to what extent can one expect teachers to be critical in ways that will promote student self-learning? Eisner* points out that criticism is the art of disclosing the salient characteristics of subject matter. The task of the critic is to describe qualities and aspects that can be located in the subject matter being criticized. Criticism is not an abstraction; it is an empirical undertaking. However, the ability to criticize is based upon the ability to perceive what is subtle, complex, and important in the subject being criticized. This ability is often called *connoisseurship,* to indicate that unless one is able to perceive subtleties and nuances, one's criticism is likely to be superficial. Thus, if critical teachers are wanted, it will be necessary to find teachers who are "connoisseurs" in their subject area, teachers who can relate the subtleties of their subjects to the knowledge that students disclose to them.

Like teaching, connoisseurship develops with experience. But also like teaching, there is an artistic, personal component of the process which cannot be generated—or, at least, which cannot be generated given the present state of knowledge. This is not to suggest that some people do not develop connoisseurship through experience and education—they certainly do. However, one rarely can discern the particular experiential and educational features that have helped a given person succeed, and one can even less directly transfer this success to others. It is, then, this artistic component that separates the exemplar from the ordinary, for connoisseurship, like artistry, is the ideal in teaching, not the commonplace.

Is it possible to readily identify teachers who have the sensitivity, values, knowledge, and connoisseurship to create the necessary educational environments and provide the appropriate criticisms to carry out critical pedagogy? I suggest that this will be a difficult search. Can the appropriate characteristics be developed in teachers? Probably, but not until better knowledge

*E. W. Eisner, *The Educational Imagination* (New York: Macmillan, 1979).

structures for how to help develop affective, artistic, and conceptual knowledge are available. If these knowledge structures have to evolve by trial and error, the wait could be lengthy.

CONCLUSION

I believe that Professor Perkinson is correct in stating that the student must be an active participant in knowledge creation. I applaud Professor Perkinson for his emphasis on the critical importance of the teacher in the educational transaction and the view of the teacher as a sensitive, informed, supportive, decision-making critic of student knowledge. I appreciate the critical reflection about educational processes that his piece provoked. He has provided a vision—dare I say, goal—of where education might venture.

However, it also is necessary to point out that education is a social institution that does not yield easily to change; since one of its prime societal functions is to support the existing social, political, and economic context, it is best thought of as a conservative institution. Moreover, the heart of the educational process, the interaction between student and teacher, is difficult to prescribe and control because it is so greatly dependent upon the uniqueness of the participants in the interaction. While I do not celebrate the current status of education and teaching, in reviewing any educational reform it is important to recognize the complexity of the classroom environment, the context of classroom teaching, and the difference between theory and practice. My comments were intended to convey these realities.

8

Critical Pedagogy and Political Power

Joel Spring
SUNY, Old Westbury

I agree with Henry Perkinson's basic framework for a critical education. What I think is missing from his argument is a clear exposition of the relationship between power and knowledge. A consideration of the connection between power and knowledge changes the nature of his argument about the evolution of knowledge, the use of competition of the marketplace to improve education, and the critical dialogue in his proposed method of instruction.

Perkinson's discussion of the evolution of knowledge rests on the assumption that evolution is progressive and that the survival of particular ideas is determined by their ability to adapt to the needs of society. I would argue that evolution is not necessarily progressive and that the survival of particular ideas is a result of power relations in society.

When most people think of evolution, they assume that survival of the fittest must mean that evolution is progressive. Of course, the first issue is the meaning of progress. For instance, evolution is not progressive for those species who do not adapt and disappear from the planet. Many people would argue that the daily destruction of species by humans, particularly in the rain forests of the world, is not a progressive act. In the framework of evolutionary theory, the destruction of these species is part of the process by which humans are adapting to their environment. Ironically, this form of adaptation could result in the disappearance of the human species. If this were to occur, then evolution would certainly not be progressive for humans.

In the framework of the above argument, the direction of human evolution is dependent on power relations among humans. The same thing is true of the evolution of knowledge. What happens to the earth's environment is dependent on the political and economic forces at work in the world. In other words, survival of the human species is dependent on decisions made by corporations, governments, and other individuals and organizations exercising power in today's world.

The evolution of knowledge is also tied to power relationships. In the western world, the Catholic church played a major role in the Middle Ages in determining what knowledge would be "fittest" for society and, of course, the church favored forms of knowledge that would enhance its power in society. In the twentieth century, governments around the world manipulate both the creation and dissemination of knowledge for the purpose of enhancing their power. Corporations have a stake in what knowledge survives. Certainly, corporations are not interested in the survival of ideas such as the importance of unions in maintaining adequate salaries for workers. In fact, corporations seem to have been fairly successful in the United States in stamping out a belief in the role of unions in improving the working and living conditions of workers.

Of course, the survival of ideas is *not* just a result of the power of elites. Perkinson gives the example of the impact of political actions by African Americans, Hispanics, and women in the 1960s and 1970s in extending the socialization function of public schools. As he points out, these groups started a political campaign to change the content of schooling because the knowledge being disseminated by the schools was sexist and racist, and, consequently, detrimental to their economic and political power. In this situation, political power, but not the power of dominant groups, resulted in changes in school knowledge.

Therefore, the knowledge that survives in the evolutionary process may not be the knowledge that is the "fittest," but it is the knowledge that survives from conflicts of power. And, of course, the surviving knowledge might not be progressive for human beings. This is particularly true in a world in which scientific knowledge has produced nuclear weapons and chemicals that may make the environment unfit for humans. Also, the social sciences may be producing the tools that would make it possible for governments to exert totalitarian control over a population by manipulation of the messages disseminated by mass media and the schools. In the case of totalitarianism, human survival might occur without human happiness.

The relationship between knowledge and power should also be considered in Perkinson's advocacy of turning schools over to the forces of the marketplace. Using an evolutionary framework, Perkinson argues, ". . . the competition in the market among the schools for clients would weed out that knowledge that is *not* worth knowing. Thus, the market would promote the evolution of the curriculum through the procedure of trial-and-error elimination" (page 75).

Before turning directly to the issue of knowledge and power in the marketplace, it is important to note that the Bush administration is advocating turning schools over to the forces of the marketplace, and at the same time, it is advocating national standards and national achievement tests. The effect of national standards for each subject matter area and national achievement tests would be to create a national curriculum. Combined with a choice plan, a national curriculum would result in schools competing to determine what method is best for achieving national standards and for preparing students for national achievement tests. In this situation, competition in the marketplace between schools would *not* eliminate knowledge that is "*not* worth knowing." The decision over what is worth knowing would be determined by the political forces determining national standards and the content of national achievement tests.

If we consider the role of the marketplace without President Bush's plan, it is still uncertain whether or not the knowledge "not worth knowing" would be weeded out. In the United States, the marketplace is not neutral. Some competitors in the marketplace have special advantages because of wealth or special connections to government. Wealth, of course, is an important ingredient in the marketplace because of the important role of advertising. Usually, more money results in better quality and increased quantity of advertising. Wealth also buys connections to political power.

In the case of schools, economic power could rule the marketplace. Currently, the Whittle Corporation is designing schools to be nationally franchised. With a choice plan it is probable that other large corporations will begin franchising schools. It is not inconceivable that a corporation such as McDonald's will franchise Ronald McDonald schools. These corporations would be advantaged in the marketplace because of their ability to buy superior advertising. In addition, since the government would still be funding and regulating schooling, these large corporations would be at an advantage over schools with fewer economic resources in dealing with the government. Large corporations would be able to hire lawyers and influence politicians so that laws and regulations would favor their schools in the competition in the marketplace.

In addition to their advantage in competing, large corporations would also be interested in disseminating knowledge that would be to their advantage. Certainly, they would want their schools to teach a form of history, economics, and political science that would protect their economic interests. Also, they would want schools to produce compliant workers who would not demand higher wages. Therefore, competition in the marketplace under current economic and political conditions might result in the survival of knowledge that is in the interests of the major corporations competing in that marketplace.

I agree with Perkinson that the individual should have the

power to decide what is worth knowing and that it should not be a decision made by politicians. But I do not see how with the great disparities in wealth in our society that people can participate equally in that decision-making process. Besides wealth enhancing opportunities in the marketplace, it also appears to be related to a person's knowledge of the options that are available. In other words, for someone to determine what is worth knowing, the person must know the range of possible knowledge. Currently, the distribution of this type of knowledge seems to vary from person to person and social class to social class.

This consideration of the role of power in the evolution of knowledge and competition in the marketplace relates directly to Perkinson's concept of a critical education. I do not disagree with Perkinson's advocacy of a critical education, but I think his concept of a critical education is limited because of a lack of consideration of the relationship between power and knowledge.

For instance, the key element in Perkinson's critical education is presentation to students of knowledge as conjectural. Perkinson writes that teachers should present the theories of experts "as imperfect conjectures of fallible human beings, conjectures that students should encounter critically" (page 59). Critical thinking about these conjectures, according to Perkinson, will help the student's knowledge to grow. Important to this form of intellectual growth is a critical dialogue between the student and sources of knowledge, including books and teachers.

Now I agree with this approach to teaching. Whenever I present material to students, I tell them not to believe anything I say—particularly, ideas that are products of research and statements by experts. I tell students that research and expert opinion are really forms of argument and that the students should engage in an argument with the material.

In addition, unlike Perkinson, I stress that knowledge is a product of social relationships. Even the scientific researcher is influenced by social events in the determination of what research should be pursued. In addition, particularly in our world, scientific research depends on political decisions about what areas should be investigated. Since World War II, the major focus of scientific research in the United States has been on military development. Of course, many consumer products were spun off from this research, but the reality is that a major part of research money has gone into military programs.

In stating that knowledge is a product of social relationships, I am also stating that knowledge is a product of the exercise of power. For instance, in the case of scientific research since World War II, a great deal of our present knowledge and world has been determined by struggles of power in international relations. We might be living in an entirely different world if the major focus of research had been on problems of medical care, nutrition, and improving the conditions of the environment. But political decisions were made not to place the major emphasis on research in these areas.

Therefore, if we just present knowledge to students as conjecture, as Perkinson recommends, we are not truly heightening their level of critical awareness. I would argue that knowledge should be presented as a product of social relationships where exercise of power is a major factor. In this way students would not only argue with the material but would also investigate why particular types of knowledge exist and not other types of knowledge. In this manner a student would truly be engaged in a critical form of education which not only would enhance her or his knowledge, but also would lead to an understanding of how knowledge is created and how it survives in human societies.

The result of this form of critical education would be not only the type of thinker desired by Perkinson but also one that understands how knowledge is used as an instrument of power and knows how to create and use knowledge for one's own objectives. In other words, one learns to shape the world according to one's desires as opposed to the desires of those who have the most power. This form of learning, I would argue, would truly be liberating.

In summary, I find most of Perkinson's argument very appealing. But his discussion of evolution, choice between schools, and critical education are limited because of a lack of consideration of the political dimensions of knowledge. Like Perkinson, I would like a world where the individual becomes the determiner of what knowledge is of most worth. In addition, I would like the individual to understand how he or she can create and exercise new knowledge. Unfortunately, achieving the type of world that both Perkinson and I would like depends on a fundamental redistribution of power in contemporary society. In fact, the control of knowledge might be key to avoiding an evolutionary process where changes in environmental conditions result in the end of the human species.

9

Critical Pedagogy and the Feminist Perspective

Joan Burstyn
Syracuse University

As a teacher educator, feminist, and historian of education, I find Henry Perkinson's book refreshing and yet passé. It's refreshing because, like a cold shower, his demand that teachers abandon goals for their students and replace them merely with an agenda to help their students' knowledge grow startles one wide awake. Here's an argument that boldly challenges existing assumptions that teachers should set goals for their students, that education has as its purpose the shaping of productive citizens, and that only by setting goals can teachers measure their effectiveness. If those of us who train teachers are to argue with Perkinson, we'll have to examine and then defend these assumptions. That might prove stimulating. Would it affect teacher education positively? I think so. Even to have faculty and students debate the issues Perkinson raises is to encourage us all to become more reflective about our practice.

At the same time, the book is passé because Perkinson accepts weathered assumptions about the neutrality of learning environments and the equal value people give to ideas. He thereby discounts the impact of class, race, and gender on education. He also fails to consider how new technologies are changing people's modes of thinking and learning.

Perkinson argues that each student, however young, has his or her own theories of how the world works and how tasks should be performed. People test the validity of their theories through the reactions of objects and people to actions based on them. Thus, through a process of "trial-and-error elimination" each person refines his or her skills and ideas. The task of a teacher is not to provide students with correct information but to create an environment conducive for students to learn about the validity of their skills and understandings.

"I am against treating education as the promotion of learning," says Perkinson. "Instead, I suggest that we consider education as growth, the growth of knowledge" (page 5). By saying this, Perkinson seems to assume that most people construe education merely as "the promotion of learning," an assumption that certainly needs defending before it is accepted. Then, in suggesting that we should construe education as "the growth of knowledge," he appears to have changed the source of agency in education from the teacher (who presumably promotes learning) to the learner (whose knowledge grows). On further examination, however, this turns out to be the case in only one arena. Perkinson describes two arenas where knowledge grows. In the first, he removes any individual, teacher or learner, from the definition of education. He does this by describing how, in this arena, the growth of knowledge inheres not in people, but in the bodies of knowledge that men and women have created. These bodies exist, he claims, because humans, unlike other animals, have the capacity to "objectify" their skills and understandings by speaking, writing, and printing them. Using a metaphor developed by Karl Popper, Perkinson describes how these bodies of human knowledge evolve:

> Like the biological bodies human beings also create—their children—these various bodies of knowledge evolve and grow—so much so that we can compose and have composed histories of the growth and development of bodies of knowledge: histories of mathematics, histories of science, etc.

> As the evolutionary epistemologists have made clear, the growth of these bodies of objective knowledge in every field follows the Darwinian process of trial-and-error elimination. (page 11)

In this arena, then, each body of knowledge men and women have created behaves, according to Perkinson, as though it were a separate, complex biological organism. I draw the reader's attention to this because I think Perkinson's use of the metaphor is not persuasive. He bases it on an interpretation of Darwinism that does not take into account the discovery of DNA and its role in providing a genetic code for developing organisms. Would it make sense for Perkinson to include in his metaphor the idea that bodies of knowledge created by humans contain within them the genetic codes needed for their own growth, independent of the humans who have developed them? It would certainly make his metaphor more exact and would strengthen his argument that bodies of knowledge grow without human agency; but I doubt that it would make sense, even though some people may believe that humans do simulate a genetic code in the design of a self-correcting computer that sends information back to their "brain" about their own malfunctioning. This information is then used by the computer to correct its own problems. Even in this case, however, it's not the body of information that creates and recreates itself; a computer does that as a result of interacting with the body of knowledge. Hence, a body of knowledge depends on an external agent for its initiation, continuation, and interpretation. Without an external agent to interact with it, whether that agent be a human or a computer, it's impossible to envision the growth of a body of knowledge, because it does not contain within itself a genetic code that influences and constrains its development.

Another way that a body of knowledge differs from a complex biological organism is that it accretes without necessarily maintaining coherence as an entity. Nor does it have boundaries except in the minds of humans who have chosen to define boundaries for it. Thus, while it is useful in a limited way to compare bodies of knowledge to complex biological organisms, I think it's misleading to assume as close a parallel between them as Perkinson does. Human agency, or the agency of a surrogate human in the form of an intelligent machine, is needed for growth to occur in a body of knowledge.

The second arena in which Perkinson embeds the growth of knowledge inheres in individuals who, according to him, only learn through the development of internal theories that they then test in the external world of the senses through a process of "trial-and-error elimination." Here, again, Perkinson applies the metaphor of evolution. In a sense its application here is more appropriate because each person is a separate, complex biological organism. On the other hand, it is only by subscribing to the belief that ontogeny follows phylogeny, which Perkinson does not seem inclined to do, that one can apply an argument about the evolution of species to the "evolution" of specific individuals.

Perkinson argues that because each person learns through a process of testing his or her individual theories against the external world, the role of the teacher is not to present "correct" knowledge, but to provide an environment where three criteria exist: students feel free to disclose their own skills and understandings; students get immediate feedback on the adequacy of their skills and understandings; and they feel enough support to "try again when the critical feedback uncovers the inadequacies in their knowledge" (page 34). Perkinson claims that in such an environment the teacher is not an authority, but merely a facilitator, "someone who can help the students uncover mistakes, errors, inadequacies, in their performances and in their understandings" (page 37). This definition of a teacher may seem familiar to many who have spent time in educating teachers. It has been a hallmark of progressive educators even though, as Perkinson points out, they have never moved as far away from traditional educators as they would like people to believe. I'm not sure, however, that Perkinson's teachers will be able to perform in the way that he would like them to because he does not take into account certain psychological and sociological phenomena that influence learners and interfere with the ability of teachers to function as he envisions.

Other scholars have pointed out, for instance, that people are in no position to accept criticism until their ideas and opinions have found confirmation and acceptance. Those involved with counseling, conflict resolution, mediation, and negotiation will attest to the necessity first to understand and accept the other's attitudes and needs before attempting to criticize them.* The task of a teacher, therefore, is more than to serve as a facilitator for the critiquing of students' skills and understandings. It is, also, to provide affirmation of students' skills and understandings, however erroneous they may appear, while at the same time introducing the idea that all skills and understandings can be improved. Perkinson would have us believe that "trial-and-error elimination" takes place in a neutral sphere, where each one of the adults with "mature" skills and understandings will give similar feedback to the learner. We know that is not true. Teachers are influenced in their interactions with students by prejudices, stereotypes, and personal preferences, as well as by the history of their relationships with each student. I shall give examples below of the influence of gender prejudice; others could identify similar prejudice with regard to race and class.

A few months ago I attended a first grade classroom where, at "today's news" time, the teacher inquired whether it was anyone's birthday. I said it was mine. When the children asked how old I was, I told them, and then I suggested, as an afterthought, that they might want to see if they could calculate in what year I'd been born. Several gave wild guesses before the teacher directed them on to other news items. Somewhile later a boy came up to me as I walked around the class. "You were born in 1944,"

*The literature on these issues spreads over several decades. See, for example, Carl Rogers's discussion of acceptance in *On Becoming a Person* (1961); Eric Berne, *Games People Play* (1964); John Holt's discussions of these issues in *How Children Fail* (1964) and *How Children Learn* (1967); Roger Fisher and William Ury, *Getting to Yes* (1981); and Mary Field Belenky, Blythe McVicker Clinchy, Nancy Rule Goldberger, and Jill Mattuck Tarule, *Women's Ways of Knowing* (1986). Uncertainty of acceptance strongly influences people's interpersonal relations as Jules Henry described in his classic, *Culture against Man* (1963): "When the personal community is unstable and must be constantly worked on and propped up, individual idiosyncracies become dangerous and must be ruled out in favor of tried and true skills that ring bells 100 per cent of the time in the endless American game of interpersonal pinball" (p. 148).

he said confidently. I shook my head no. He looked very puzzled as he went away. Then a girl came to me and asked shyly, "Were you born in 1956?" "No," I replied. She went back to her seat, disappointed. She never came forward again. Only the boy persisted with his solutions: "1947?" "1938?" "1920?" he asked at intervals during the morning. The teacher saw these interactions but did not offer any comments. However, the boy needed more feedback than I was giving him if he was to solve the problem. His theory was too naive to solve the problem; he needed some clues about how to improve it. After lunch, I suggested this to the teacher. She smiled: "I met with him while he was eating lunch and explained how he could work out the right answer." She explained that the boy was very smart at mathematics and needed that kind of stimulus. I was pleased, but only later, after I had left the classroom, did I realize that both she and I had responded only to the most persistent inquirer who happened, not surprisingly given our society's socialization patterns, to be a boy. The girl, who had as much need as the boy for feedback on her theories, had not received any personal attention from either of us. And indeed there may have been others in the class who were too unsure of themselves even to venture forward who also needed help with their theories. My own sensitivity to the inequity came too late for me to take any remedial action. Another example from a university: A male statistics teacher is asked a question by a female student. He replies that the question is too complex to explain at the moment and continues his presentation. A few minutes later a male student rephrases the question asked by the female student. The teacher immediately gives him a lengthy explanation. Variations of these instances may take place hundreds of times during a female student's school and university life, giving her a very different vision of her ability to test her knowledge than is provided her male peers.*

A question of great moment to teachers is how long to accept "erroneous" skills and understandings before introducing any

*A discussion of similar issues entitled "Feminist Analyses of Gender and Schooling" may be found in Kathleen Weiler, *Women Teaching for Change* (New York: Bergin & Garvey Publishers, 1988), chap. 2.

critique of them—how to enable students to become "reflective" about what they know how to do and what they understand. Outsiders might ask, at what age is it appropriate to begin the process of critiquing and in what way is it to be done? These are questions to which Perkinson gives scant attention. I had the impression that the students he refers to are high school students at the least, and probably college students. But high school students will not flourish in the critical environment he describes if they have not had practice at an earlier age of dealing reflectively with their knowledge. Thus, at what age should children learn reflection in action, as Donald Schön would call it, and how should they learn it?* The topic becomes the more important because we know that insecure people tend to be the most rigid in their beliefs and opinions. If that is so, how does one provide an open environment in which criticism may flourish for children whose security has already been undermined by their life at home? Surely in those cases, we might argue, the first and most important task of the teacher is to confirm the skills and understandings children bring with them to school in the expectation that by so doing she or he will make the child more secure and thus able to tolerate the uncertainty that criticism brings with it.†

However, studies of the ways schools help reproduce social relations, particularly with regard to race, class, and gender, suggest there are sociological and psychological reasons why teachers find it easy to affirm the skills and understandings of some students but difficult to affirm the skills and understandings of others.‡ The fact that I, a feminist, was blind to my own gender

*See Donald Schön, *The Reflective Practitioner* (New York: Basic Books, Inc., 1983).

†With regard to affirming the understandings children bring to school with them, Barbara Finkelstein argues that in the eighteenth and nineteenth centuries the process of reading aloud in class was usually one of self-affirmation for upper- and middle-class children who heard their parents read books aloud at home. But reading aloud was a process that alienated lower-class children from their parents, who did not know how to read. [See Barbara Finkelstein, ed., *Regulated Children, Liberated Children* (New York: Psychohistory Press, 1979), chap. 6.]

‡See, for instance, the works discussed in Weiler, *Women Teaching for Change.* Another fruitful way to examine the dilemmas raised for teachers by their own belief structures is presented in Ann Berlak and Harold Berlak, *Dilemmas of Schooling* (New York: Methuen, 1981).

discrimination in the incident described above suggests to me that the influence of socialization on the way adults relate to children is very strong. Scholars of social reproduction theory have pointed out that education tends to reproduce the power structures of the existing society. Individual children may resist the power structure, or they may adapt to it, sometimes for reasons quite different from those put forward by teachers.* Nevertheless, they do not test their theories in a neutral space. They do not find that each skill or each understanding they express is accorded equal respect by the adults who examine them. Perkinson seems to ignore the unequal power that exists between adult and child, teacher and student, as well as power differences based on class, race, and gender.

He also speaks as though teaching and learning will continue as they have in the past. I doubt that. We are on the cusp of a world that provides new ways of learning and new understandings of the universe.† So both skills and understandings are changing. What is "the past" when we can recreate it on film as we wish it had been, not as it "really" was? What is the meaning of death when I can watch an interview with Einstein made many years ago and, using a computer keyboard to write them out, have him answer my questions, today, now, his face close up and he is speaking only to me from the screen? Or when, on a TV ad, I can see Elton John and Humphrey Bogart talking to one another across time and space? There was a time when only those scientists who had microscopes and telescopes were privileged to see worlds they had to take on faith—faith that the technology in their hands was producing "true" results because they had no way to verify what they saw through "trial-and-error elimination" using the naked eye. Now, through a combination

*See, for example, Paul Willis, *Learning to Labor* (New York: Columbia University Press, 1977).

†Popular books such as Alvin Toffler's *Future Shock* (1970) and *Power Shift* (1990); Stanley M. Davis, *Future Perfect* (1987); and John Naisbitt and Patricia Aburdene, *Megatrends 2000* (1990), portray the changes taking place in commerce and industry. Shoshana Zuboff's *In the Age of the Smart Machine* (New York: Basic Books, 1988) gives a scholarly analysis of life in several industries at a moment of change to the use of new information technology.

of video, film, and computers we have placed the power to create a new reality in the hands of many people. Scientists, perhaps more particularly than many others in society, have to take certain things on faith. It follows from this discussion that not all knowledge is acquired through "trial-and-error elimination." And if, as Perkinson suggests, education is the growth of knowledge, what is meant by knowledge has changed beyond recognition in the information age.* Teachers have to provide environments where children may safely learn the practice of discovery in areas the teachers themselves may never have encountered before. According to Sylvia Engdahl, even the metaphors we use to describe the universe are changing, so that children's awareness of their place in it is very different from that of most adults today.† Does "trial-and-error elimination" really take place, then, in the classroom? Which interactions should children take most into account, those with their peers who share their view of the universe or those with "knowledgeable" adults who do not? Which interactions are the more valuable for learning, those with machines or those with people?

The new meanings of reality seem to me the greatest challenge to educators in the future. I would argue that new technologies "work" for those who believe their power, and that learning through a process of "trial-and-error elimination" depends on one's faith that the technology one is using provides real data, not data that are artifacts of the technology itself. That being so, it's not clear to me that the growth of knowledge depends solely on "trial-and-error elimination"; it depends also on the development of faith, in the tools we use and in the understandings we create.

*Ann DeVaney Becker in "Picture as Visual Text," *Educational Considerations* 10, no. 2 (Spring 1983): 30–32, discusses the developing critical literature in film and video. I have raised some of the issues relating to new perceptions of reality in Joan N. Burstyn, ed., "The Challenge to Education from New Technology," *Preparation for Life? The Paradox of Education in the Late Twentieth Century* (Philadelphia: Falmer Press, 1986).

†See Sylvia Engdahl, "The Mythic Role of Space Fiction," *Journal of Social and Biological Structures* 13, no. 4 (1990): 292 ff.

10

Reply to My Critics

Henry Perkinson

My editor, Lane Akers, suggested that this book be published along with some critical responses to it, together with my reply. He thought this was in keeping with the critical approach I advocate. It is. Moreover, participating in this exercise, I experienced, once again, how critical dialogue enhances one's understanding. For by engaging the arguments of my critics, I have come to understand better what I was trying to say, and to recognize some of the mistakes I made in the text. So this format illustrates the approach I advocate and, at the same time, allows me to explain it—one more time.

I

My starting point is human fallibility. Almost all I have to say follows from, or is intimated by, acceptance of the condition of human fallibility. Thus, if human beings are fallible, then it seems obvious that we ought not construe education as a process of transmission. For when a teacher—who is, of course, a fallible human being—tells a student what is correct, true, or good, that teacher is merely telling the student what he, or she, or someone, *believes* to be correct, true, or good. This makes teaching an authoritarian activity and converts education into indoctrination—a fate, I assume, we want to avoid.

Since human fallibility means that our knowledge is never perfect, I recommend that teachers abandon all attempts to transmit knowledge to students. Most teachers find this difficult to do, entrapped as they are in the notion that we receive knowledge from without. These teachers believe students are receptors of knowledge; hence, they conclude, teachers *must* be transmitters. Thus, even though these teachers may agree that human knowledge is imperfect, they cannot accept any alternative to their conception of education as a process of transmission. In opposition to these transmission teachers, I have maintained that we do not receive knowledge, but rather—as proposed by such disparate theorists as Jean Piaget, B. F. Skinner, and Karl Popper—we create knowledge, or construct it. We are creators, not receptors. Indeed, this *is* why human knowledge is imperfect: it is the construction of fallible creators.

In addition to human knowledge being imperfect, there is another conclusion to be drawn from our condition of fallibility, which is that human knowledge can always improve, always get better—continually grow. And this, I suggest, offers the possibility of an alternative conception of education: education is the growth of knowledge.

Interestingly enough, teachers who construe education as a process of transmission have no trouble accommodating the conception that education is growth, simply because they view growth as accretion: the student's knowledge grows, these teachers believe, as the result of accumulating more and more of the knowledge transmitted to them.

Yet while sand dunes do grow by accretion, knowledge does not. For like everything else humans create—social, political, economic institutions; artifacts; art—knowledge grows through the procedure of critical selection, or trial-and-error elimination. We create something—a theory, a skill, an artifact, an art object, a policy, a procedure, a practice, an arrangement. Then we uncover the inadequacies—mistakes, problems—it contains. This provokes us to modify or refine the theory, skill, artifact, artwork, policy, practice, procedure, or arrangement—in light of the uncovered inadequacies in it. This is how the things we create, including our knowledge, grow or get better: through trial-and-error elimination.

Joan Burstyn, in her commentary, maintains that the emergence of new electronic technology throws into doubt whether or not our knowledge still grows, or will continue to grow, in this way. She may be correct, but she presents no counterexamples that refute the claim that knowledge grows through trial-and-error elimination. I would contend that electronic technology facilitates the growth of knowledge by enhancing the procedures of trial-and-error elimination. Through electronic media, we can make trial conjectures never possible before, while at the same time, these media expand our ability to uncover errors. (I have elaborated this in the case of television in my *Getting Better: Television and Moral Progress.**)

II

This conception of how knowledge grows is based on the evolutionary epistemology of Karl Popper, who has pointed out that we can facilitate the growth of knowledge through criticism. In his commentary, Joel Spring questions whether evolution is truly a progressive phenomena. This question assumes that there is some criterion of progress other than survival. Darwinism does not make this assumption. Rather, the argument goes, those species that do not survive (natural selection) are less fit than those that do. Likewise with knowledge, those theories that do not survive (criticism) are less fit than those that do.

I applied Popper's evolutionary epistemology both to the growth of subject matter fields and to the growth of personal knowledge. In her comments on what I said about the former,

*(New Brunswick, N.J.: Transaction Publishers, 1991).

Joan Burstyn correctly points out that I failed to indicate the role of human agency in the evolution of such knowledge. I agree with her: subject matter does not evolve on its own; it must be criticized.

My main focus was on the growth of personal knowledge, specifically the growth of the student's knowledge, which I take to be the teacher's primary concern. Here, the most important point, as Joan Burstyn highlights, is that the growth of the student's knowledge is up to the student—it is the student who improves his or her knowledge. The role of the teacher is simply to facilitate.

The primary function of the teacher, as I see it, is to be a critic—to help students uncover what's wrong with their present knowledge. To carry this out, teachers must construct an educative environment. This consists of three aspects: first, it is an environment that will educe the student's present knowledge, an environment wherein the student will feel free to disclose that knowledge; second, it must be an environment that provides critical feedback to the student's present knowledge—this feedback can come from the teacher, from other students, or from specially prepared materials; third, it must be a supportive environment so that students will accept the criticisms (those that they cannot refute) of their present knowledge and proceed to eliminate their errors.

From the criticism Joan Burstyn raised, I now realize that I did not sufficiently stress the importance of creating a supportive environment. It is, I think, the first order of business for the teacher, for if students do not feel supported, criticism will not provoke them to eliminate errors in their present knowledge; criticism will not, therefore, facilitate growth. The teacher must give students what Carl Rogers calls "unconditional positive regard," so that students will believe, as A. S. Neill put it: "the teacher is on their side." But I do not agree with Joan Burstyn's conclusion that this means that the teacher must "confirm the skills and understandings children bring with them to school" (page 107). I think it is very important to distinguish between students and their knowledge, and to confirm, or validate, or support, *them,* not their knowledge. By supporting *them,* I mean supporting them as agents, as creators of knowledge who can always improve their skills, continually create better understandings. The praise that teachers give to students, and I do think we should shower our students with praise, should be for doing better, never for being correct.

III

Although creating a supportive environment is the first order of business of the teacher, the primary function is to create a *critical* environment—an environment that provides students with critical feedback. This is why I call my approach the critical approach. I think that this critical approach can be readily adopted by teachers who work in the schools and classrooms that presently exist. The fundamental changes called for are conceptual: first, the critical approach requires that teachers have a new conception of education—as a procedure of growth through trial-and-error elimination; second, a new conception of the student—as a creator of knowledge; third, a new conception of the role of the teacher—as a critic, not a transmitter; and fourth, a new conception of the subject matter—as didactic material to help students improve their present knowledge, not as material to be "learned."

Peter Airasian, in his critical response, wisely raises questions about the critical approach in light of the realities of teaching. He correctly points out that some aspects of the present arrangements in schools—such as standardized evaluation—are quite incompatible with the critical approach. In this matter, I think a strategy is called for—the strategy of experimentation. That is, teachers who wish to adopt the critical approach can agree to have their students evaluated by standardized tests and, furthermore, agree to have those results compared with the results attained by students taught in the traditional way. My, perhaps utopian, hope is that such experiments will, in time, reveal that the critical approach does facilitate growth, and, therefore, people will conclude we have no need for standardized evaluations predicated on educational "goals." Instead of setting goals, we need to set what I called agendas—specifically identified areas of the student's present knowledge that are targeted to be improved. This strategy of experimentation can probably be used in dealing with other existing practices that are incompatible with the critical approach. I see experimentation as a way to get a fair tryout and eventual acceptance of the critical approach.

There are other arrangements present in our schools today—testing and grading, for example—that are not incompatible with the critical approach, but do present obstacles in carrying it out. Yet I think these can be overcome by recasting the existing practices in ways that further the critical approach. Thus, in the matter of tests, all tests should be cast as diagnostic—tests to ascertain the inadequacies in students' present knowledge; in the matter of grades, all grades should be based on the diminution of errors, or inadequacies in the student's work. This recasting should be carried out by those best suited to do it: by teachers and administrators who subscribe to the critical approach.

I hope these points satisfy some of Peter Airasian's concerns about the realities of teaching, especially in the matter of evaluation. He also raised two other concerns: will students engage in this process of trial-and-error elimination? Are teachers up to conducting the critical approach?

At the risk of sounding glib, I would say that students already do engage in the procedure of trial-and-error elimination—for this *is* how their knowledge grows, and we do know that it does grow, although teachers do not always facilitate this procedure. The basis for my saying this, as Peter Airasian recognizes, is the fact that human beings seek order, or, as I prefer to state it: disorder is aversive to us. From Aristotle to Piaget, theorists have pointed out that humans seek intellectual homeostasis, or cognitive equilibrium—we avoid, or try to escape, contradictions, or cognitive disequilibration. This is probably the outcome of our evolutionary history, since organisms that tolerated or accepted contradictions simply could not have survived. (Imagine accepting the statement: "The pool of water you are about to dive into is/is not two feet deep.")

It is true that students may be frightened or angered by the critical approach because the classroom environment is not sufficiently free or supportive, but this points to the importance of Peter Airasian's concern about whether or not teachers could create what I have called an educative environment. Can ordinary teachers carry out the critical approach? I think they can, and I think they should use it at every level of schooling. Some teachers will, of course, be "naturals," while others will only acquire the requisite skills through painful trial-and-error elimination. I realize that what I have presented remains quite abstract and theoretical. I think it is the practicing teacher who must work out many of the practical problems my critics have pointed to—a practicing teacher who understands and accepts the critical approach. The crux of the matter, I repeat, is the conceptual outlook of the teacher: the teacher's conception of the educational transaction, and of the role of the teacher, the student, and the subject matter in that transaction. Once the teacher subscribes to such a conceptualization as I have described above, he or she can work out the methods, strategies, procedures, moves, and practices that will construct an environment that will facilitate the growth of the student's knowledge.

Joan Burstyn points to another set of potential problems: those psychological and sociological difficulties teachers will confront in carrying out the critical approach. Her example of her own insensitivities in providing critical feedback to a male student, but not to a female student, graphically portrays this difficulty. My suggestion for dealing with these kinds of difficulties is to have teachers apply the critical approach to their own teaching performance. This means they will need critics. Joan Burstyn reports that she became critically conscious of her own insensitivity toward the female student, but most of us need outside help, external critics. Japanese teachers have already developed a way of doing this. In Japan, teachers are helped to improve their teaching performance by means of collaborative critical discussions with one another.* American teachers could incorporate this practice.

*See James Stigler and Harold Stevenson, "How Asian Teachers Polish Each Lesson to Perfection," *American Educator* (Spring 1991): 12–46.

IV

In addition to the question "What are teachers for?" my book contains conjectures about the question "What's worth knowing?" If we take human fallibility seriously, then we must conclude that we do not know what knowledge is of most worth—not for ourselves, nor for others, either. Yet schools must have a course of study. So what are fallible educators to do? What subjects should be taught? What kinds of intellectual growth should teachers facilitate?

My suggestion was, and is, to take this question out of the political arena, where it is usually decided by contending forces, and put it into the market. That is, I suggested that parents and students should be able to choose among different schools that offer different courses of study. I fear that I failed to stress that this procedure would not decide what's worth knowing, but rather would simply indicate what is *not* worth knowing: those courses of study that had no takers would be the ones the market has decided are not worth knowing. The necessary precondition for this market approach is that anyone or any group would be free to open a school and students would be free to attend the school of their (or their parents') choice, and to leave it for another if not satisfied.

Joel Spring has criticized this proposal, arguing that the inequities in the distribution of power in our society will prevent free choice from taking place. Thus, he points out that some groups will have more funding for their schools, as well as superior advertising. This is undoubtedly correct, but his conclusion does not follow. Unless people are satisfied with what they purchase, they will not continue as customers, especially if they can purchase from an alternative vendor. Thus, in the competitive open market, the big three automotive manufacturers in Detroit, in spite of abundant funding and superior advertising, are losing customers to Japanese automakers. Analogously, so long as people are free to choose not to go to a specific school, they will not be forced to subscribe to decisions made by powerful others about what's worth knowing. So long as students are free to exit, then those schools that inadequately serve the interests of the student and/or of the parents will fail. The courses of study they offer will not be worth knowing.

As I understand Joel Spring's paper, he has an answer to the question "What's worth knowing?" He suggests that what I call the critical approach should include "consideration of the relationship between power and knowledge" (page 98). He wants teachers to present knowledge "as a product of social relationships where exercise of power is a major factor" (page 99). By doing this, he says, teachers will help students "truly heighten . . . their level of critical awareness." For, he says, by "investigat[ing] why particular types of knowledge exist and not other types of knowledge," they would come to understand "how knowledge is created, and how it survives in human societies" (page 99). In short, Joel Spring proposes that what's worth knowing for our students is to get them to understand that the existing courses of study offered in our schools are there as a result of the efforts of powerful groups in society to buttress and retain their power.

I think that doing what Joel Spring recommends would corrupt the critical approach I advocate. This approach, once again, is based on the acceptance of human fallibility, which means that we cannot know with certainty why the existing knowledge was created, nor what might have been created in its stead. To claim that the possession of such knowledge should be the outcome of the critical approach is to reject human fallibility and to fail to understand the critical approach. The critical approach does not lead to certain knowledge, ever. It simply reveals our ignorance, helps make us aware that what we thought was so is not. Of course, we can make conjectures about why knowledge was created and why it survives, and such conjectures can be presented to students as conjectures to engage critically. This would be a critical approach.

I want to thank the three critics who participated in this critical dialogue. They have helped to improve my understanding of what I have written and, I hope, helped me to explain it better to other readers. The task before all of us is to ensnare more people into this critical dialogue. Education cannot but improve if more of us, as Joan Burstyn put it, "become more reflective about our practice."